The City Of
Westwood, Kansas
50 Years
Of Progress

Compiled and
Edited by

Gene Culbertson

Joe Vaughan Associates
Communications Services and Publishing
P.O. Box 8524
Prairie Village, Kansas 66208-0524

Library of Congress Catalog Number 566 369
ISBN: 0-963686-3-4-8

Printed in the United States of America
by Publishing Specialists, Inc., Shawnee, KS 66216
FIRST EDITION 1999

To obtain copies of the book, contact:
City Clerk
City of Westwood
4700 Rainbow Boulevard
Westwood, KS 66205
(913) 362-1550 • Fax: (913) 362-3308

Contents

PREFACE

By Gene Culbertson

This book is dedicated to the past, present and future citizens of the City of Westwood, Kansas.

I send a warm thanks to the citizens who helped to make the publication of the history of our city possible. Your memories in the articles furnished added what was needed to cover the beginning years. Your interest and cooperation have made this book more complete.

I want to thank the Johnson County Sun Newspaper for being so willing to share articles and pictures.

I cannot begin to thank Councilman Jim Donovan enough for the many telephone calls and trips he made to gather information and photographs. He gave me a sense of security and assurance as the history book was being put together. Even his trying to teach me how to use a computer — that in itself was quite a feat!

As this is a beginning of the recorded history of our city in book form, there is hope that others in the future will continue to keep track of our happening to put together a second book.

Happy 50th Anniversary!

Gene Culbertson

Gene Culbertson

Former Westwood City Clerk
and City Councilwoman

Westwood City Hall
4700 Rainbow
Westwood, KS 66205

*As seen from
47th & Rainbow*

*Ground Breaking
Ceremony,
1990*

*City Hall
Interior Courtyard*

WESTWOOD

Foreword

An anniversary is a special celebration, one which includes the elements of time, relationships, commitment, challenges, and triumph. Our Westwood Fifty years of history resembles a quilt. made up of many individuals and their stories, yet connected by the fabric that makes us a neighborhood and a community.

Our thanks go to the many residents whose efforts have gotten us this far, and especially to those who have shared their experiences in this volume.

And we wish Godspeed to those who will move us toward the future, making Westwood an even better place to live, work, and raise families.

Happy Anniversary!!

William L. Kostar
Mayor

BRIEF HISTORY OF THE STATE OF KANSAS

1682 Kansas included in French claim to Louisiana region by LaSalle.

1723 Sieur De Bourgmount marched from Fort Orleans, at the mouth of the Missouri River, to this area.

1803 Louisiana Purchase, the area became known as the Louisiana Territory.

1812 Missouri Territory created.

1821 Missouri became a state and Kansas became a part of the unorganized territory.

1830 The original Shawnee Mission was established by the Methodists near Turner and moved to Shawnee in 1839. It served several thousand Indian Youths in training for manual and domestic arts.

1854 Territory of Kansas organized (Kansas - Nebraska Bill by Congress). The territory included an area extending from Missouri to the Rocky Mountains. The legislation also provided for the establishment of counties, including Wyandotte and Johnson (named after Rev. Thomas Johnson, founder of the Shawnee Mission.) (53rd and Mission Road).

1855 Capital of the Territory of Kansas established at Shawnee Mission, where first Territorial Legislature met.

1859 The Wyandotte constitution adopted by Territory of Kansas.

1860 Kansas admitted as a State.

1912 Women's suffrage in Kansas.

BRIEF HISTORY OF NORTHEAST JOHNSON COUNTY

Native Roots

Property located at 4958 Rainbow was built and lived in by a descendant of the Shawnee Indian tribe. It was a part of the Indian grant of Mr. Swatzell's great, great grandfather, Capt. Joseph Parks, received from the US government almost 250 years ago. He was head chief of the Shawnee, an interpreter for government and a shrewd landowner. When Mr. Parks arrived in this area about 1833, he brought his wife. The story is she was an Indian woman known as "Olathe" meaning "Beautiful." Some stories say that in her memory the City of Olathe was named.

Many facts about Captain Parks are hazy, particularly those about his origin – where and when he was born and how much Indian blood he had. The inscription on his monument in 1794 said "Captain" Joe Parks, onetime head chief of the Shawnee Indians, was born, yet there is no data found as to his origin. But it is said of him, as of many of the progressive Shawnee Chiefs, that there was a strong infusion of white blood in his veins.

During the Seminoles war the government recruited a company of Shawnees, which served during the campaign under the leadership of Joseph Parks, at which time he acquired the title of Captain. He died April 3, 1859, at the age of 65.

After his death, the land passed on to his heirs, first to his daughter, Sally Rogers, then to her two daughters Rebecca and Catherine. Catherine married John R. Swatzell and stayed on the land. The land was sold off through the years and John Swatzell's three sons, Charles, Elmer, and John A. Swatzell inherited sizeable parcels.

The three had dairy farms through the early half of this century. Local residents who grew up in this area recall the cold spring running west of Rainbow where milk cans were kept cool and fresh and where watercress was abundant. The Swatzell brothers built their homes from natural rock in the ledges along the creek that ran through Westwood Hills, a part of their dairy land.

Cap't Joseph Parks was an early settler of what would become Westwood, Kansas. This is a photo of Parks' grandson John and Bertie Swatzell and great-grandson, Jack.

Catherine Parks Swatzell   John Thomas Swatzell

John A. Swatzell built the house at 4958 Rainbow Boulevard where his son Jack lived until his death about 1910. It is made of thick rock walls that kept it cool in summer and warm in winter. The interior woodwork is cherry. The home is at this date, 1998, occupied by one of Jack Swatzell's sons, Robert Swatzell and his family.

Great-granddson Jack lived in this house on the nowthwest corner of 50th Street and Rainbow Boulevard, married, and raised two sons. The home is 100 years old and remains in the Swatzell family

WESTWOOD - THE JEWEL OF NORTHEAST JOHNSON COUNTY

It was during the years following World War I and the Great Depression that business interests began to be actively aware of the opportunity offered in northeast Johnson County, and housing developers started casting eyes toward this section. Then came the World War II, when all was forgotten except all our efforts for victory.

A group of citizens of this area (Westwood) organized the Hudson Mission Homes Association. Mrs. J.V. Dunn 2714 W. 49th Street was responsible for getting the organization underway. Many hours were spent getting utilities, streets, sewers, etc. to the area. Mr. Murry Maxwell was appointed president of the organization, Robert L. Newman, M. D. secretary, and Al Armstrong, treasurer.

When the war ended, the rush to Northeast Johnson County was resumed and soon mushroomed into a movement for a larger scale than had ever been envisioned by those who had first seen the area's possibilities.

Very shortly the increase in population made it evident that the people could be served by establishing their own urban government and the first of the small cities came into being. The City of Leawood was first in 1948.

Westwood's Mayor and City Councilmen, left to right: Glenn Myers, Lloyd J. Svoboda, Thomas C. Hurst (now resigned), Mayor B. J. Lutz, Norman E. Gaar, Police Judge, and George K. Keller
The council is shown following a change in mayors during a November 1962 meeting.

Because the Homes Association did not have the authority to enforce or make laws, they decided to get the City incorporated.

Contact was made through the Law Offices of Payne and Jones in Olathe. The procedure necessary to form the incorporation was spelled out by Howard Payne, attorney-at-law. The Homes Association asked Mr. Payne if he would represent them. He suggested that a special fund be established for the expenses of incorporation. Mr. Martell was appointed as treasurer of this fund and the expenses of bonding Mr. Martell were to be paid by the Homes Association.

The residents of the incorporated area were to be contacted by the board of the Homes Association and asked to donate the sum of $5.00. Mr. Payne's fee for this service was $1,000.00.

The subject of what name to give the city came up. At that time, the area east of State Line was called Westwood, Missouri. It was an area of good standing, and the former Hudson Elementary School had been renamed Westwood View. Plus the prefix "Westwood" appeared before the names of several subdivisions in the Hudson-Mission Homes Association area: Westwood Court, Westwood Estates, and Westwood Orchards. There being no Westwood, Kansas, that name was adopted.

Petition Committees were being formed to obtain signatures requesting the County and State grant Incorporation as a third class city. The necessary documents were filed with the County Commissioners on May 5, 1949. On June 3, 1949 the County Commissioner Board met and found the documents to be reasonable and to allow the County Clerk to spread the order of this Board upon its records that the request has been granted.

In accordance with laws of the State of Kansas, a Special Election was held on June 30, 1949, at the Westwood View

School, Johnson County, Kansas. The polls were opened at 8:00 am and closed at 6:00 pm. Leonard White, County Clerk, swore the Election Board on June 29, 1949, at the Westwood View School, at 8:00 pm. A Board of Canvassers consisting of Vivian Dunn, Dona B. Limburg, and Bernice H. Hutcheson was appointed. Bernice H. Hutcheson was elected Clerk of the Board of Canvassers, which met at 2:00 P.M. on July 1, 1949. Margaret Hedman, Judge of the Election Board, presented the returns of the Election to the Board of Canvassers. A canvass of the votes showed that the following candidates received the highest number of votes for each office:

For Mayor	Murry W. Maxwell	287 votes
Police Judge	George C. Hurst	291 "
Councilman	John C. Hearst	275 "
	John Kesl, Jr.	279 "
	Arthur V. Shaw	277 "
	James V. Suddath	266 "
	George W. Woster	267 "

Westwood Elementary School, circa 1946

Robert E. Hays, Notary Public, swore the above officers of the City of Westwood, Kansas, into office on July 1, 1949. Westwood's boundaries were 47th street on the north, Rainbow Boulevard on the east, Mission Road on the west, and Johnson Drive (present day Shawnee Mission Parkway) and the rear property line of the houses along 51st Street Terrace on the south. On May 30, 1960, the County Commission requested Westwood to annex Westport Annex (present day 47th Terrace and 48th Street) and Westport View (present day 47th Place) from Rainbow Boulevard to State Line. At the time of annexation, Westport View was undeveloped and zoned for business.

On July 12, 1949, Mr. Curtis F. Snyder was appointed the City Clerk. The office was located in his home. Later the city managed to lease a small building from Logan Moore Lumber Company on the south side of 47th Street.

In 1961 the City Clerk's Office as well as the police office moved into the basement of the Husdon Oil Company building located at 4724 Rainbow. In 1970, arrangements were made to lease the second floor of Dr. Lee Patrick's Office Building at 4800 Rainbow.

REASONS FOR CHOICE OF NAME "WESTWOOD, KANSAS"

1. The school within our area is known as "Westwood View" and is commonly referred to throughout the township as Westwood School.
2. The prefix "Westwood" appears before the names of several subdivisions in the Hudson-Mission Homes' Association area:
   Westwood Court
   Westwood Estates
   Westwood Orchards
3. A church within our boundaries, under construction during the time of our incorporation, was known as Westwood Christian Church.
4. There is no Westwood, Kansas.
Rebuttal For Opposition To The Similarity Between Westwood and Westwood Hills
1. Two Kansas Cities
2. All of the Homes' Associations, businesses and clubs with the prefix Mission.

Aerial view of the soon-to-be city of Westwood as housing and commercial development began, circa 1940.

Map labels (City of Westwood, Kansas — Platted Subdivisions):

KANSAS CITY KANSAS

WYANDOTTE COUNTY
JOHNSON COUNTY

KANSAS CITY MISSOURI

Unnamed

Palmer Heights — Ackerman

Westport View — Woodside Club Complex — Westport View

Mission Circle — Belini Place

Unnamed

Fulton Place

Mission View — Mission Court

Swatzell Place — Magnolia Place

McQuary Plaza

47th ST. TERRACE

Westport Annex

Shawnee Park — Westport Orchard

Pin Oak Court — Westwood Court

Yates — Westwood Orchard

WESTWOOD HILLS KANSAS

Wylie Speer Addition

Unnamed

Swatzell View

Fromholtz Addition

Coronado Addition — Lloyd Avenue West

Belinder Addition

Unnamed

Lloyd Avenue West

Biggerstaff Heights

Swatzell Addition

Holmesland

Lockwood Court

CITY OF WESTWOOD, KANSAS

Platted Subdivisions

Holmesland Court — Holmesland — Resurvey Lot 16

Holmesland — Westwood Estates

Old Mission Estates — Resurvey Lot 15

Klassen Place

Holmesland

FAIRWAY KANSAS

Mills

ROELAND PARK KANSAS — MISSION ROAD

MISSION WOODS KANSAS

STATE LINE ROAD

RAINBOW AVE.

BELINDER AVE. — BOOTH AVE. — ADAMS STREET

FAIRWAY PARKWAY — U.S. HWY 56

graphic scale in feet   0   200   400   600   800

STREETS

There are a total of 8.6 miles of streets in the City of Westwood. This is comprised of 2.4 miles of arterial, 1.2 miles of collectors, and 5.0 miles of local streets. The streets are all paved. Shawnee Mission Parkway and Rainbow Blvd. are the only streets in the city which have four lanes of pavement.

SIDEWALKS

In 1970 there was 15,555 feet of sidewalks in the city. There are sidewalks on both sides of Rainbow Blvd. the west side of Belinder, the south side 50th Street both sides of 50th Terrace from mid-block east to Belinder, the south side of 51 Terrace from Mission Road to Belinder Road , the north side of 51st Terrace from Belinder to 51st Street which continues along 51st Street to Rainbow Blvd. A short street extends along north side of 49th Street a distance approximately 150 feet west of Rainbow Blvd. Sidewalks have recently been placed on east side of Adams street between 48th street Terrace and 50th street which brings the total to 16,540 feet.

Internationally famous for fine foods. Our Specialties - Fried Chicken and Steak Dinners

GREEN PARROT INN, 52nd St. and State Line, Kansas City, Mo.

The Green Parrot Inn at 52nd St. and State Line, circa 1940

Our Specialty - Fried Chicken Dinners

GREEN PARROT INN - 52nd St. and State Line - Kansas City, Mo.

The Green Parrot Inn, circa 1950

NOTEABLE BUSINESS THROUGHOUT OUR HISTORY

Business- Bldg. home 1952
> Mission Road:
>> St. Agnes Kindergarten
>> Olivet Baptist Church-4901 Mission Rd.
>> 7-11 Store
>> Small Tool Manufacture
>> Service Station
> 47th Street from Mission-East to Rainbow
>> Small Bldg.-3033 W. 47th City Hall (owned by Logan Moore, large storage for lumber. Their main office was located on North corner of 47th and Mission Rd.)
>> Small offices
>> Laundry
>> Culligan Water
>> Service Station-Auto service 47th and Rainbow
>> Gas Company
>> Lumber Company
>> Manufacturing Rep.
>> Import Inn- Small Car.
>> Phillips Service Station-47th and Rainbow
> East Side of Rainbow going South
>> Youth For Christ-Office and Print Shop
>> Cleaners
>> Plumbing
>> FMA Animal Hospital 47th Terr. and Rainbow
>> Behind-Linen Shop
> West Side of Rainbow going South
>> Hudson Oil
>> Rainbow Nursery-4740 Rainbow
>> (opened 12/1944)
>> Behind (Hudson School)
>> Dr. Patrick's Office Bldg.
>> Montiel Grocery
>> Shelly Service Station
>> Office Equipment Bldg.
>> Fisca Oil Co.
>> Parking lot
>> Westwood Christian Church-5050 Rainbow
>> Service Station-corner of Shawnee Mission Pkwy. and Rainbow. (Conoco)
> Going West on Shawnee Mission Pkwy
>> Hallmark
>> Shopping Strip
>>> Roberts Liquor
>>> Insurance Office
>>> Barber Shop
>>> Doctor Office
>>> Beauty Shop
>>> A & P Store

Shopping Strip (Cont.)
> Regan Hamburger
> Car Wash
> Farmer's Market
> King's Hamburger
> Cousin Furniture-Shawnee Mission Pkwy and Belinder
East Side of Belinder Going North
> Cleaners
> Dental Offices
> Hardware
> Insurance
> KMBC Radio Station-50th and Belinder
Going East on 50th Street
> Westwood View Elementary School

Schools-
Westwood View
Olivet Baptist Church School
Shawnee Mission Christian which is now Mission Oaks
  Christian –an elementary school
Old Mission Jr. High
Shawnee Mission North High School
Available- St. Agnes; Bishop Miege H. S.;
St. Agnes Kindergarten

Churches-
Westwood Christian
Olivet Baptist Church
St. Agnes, Roeland Park
Westwood Lutheran, Mission Woods

Parks-
Westwood Park (50th St. and Rainbow)
Mini-Park (47th Terr. off Rainbow-East)
Mini-Park (47th Terr. corner on Belinder)

Services Provided-
Consolidated School District #512
Johnson County Consolidated Fire District #2
Johnson County Library System
Johnson County Water District #1
Johnson County Water Waste
Johnson County Transportation
K. C. Power and Light
> Gas Service
> Southwestern Bell Telephone Co.
> Deffenbaugh Disposal Services

Hudson Oil Property

Hudson Oil Company Building, which housed company personnel covering the consular offices for representatives of Columbia and Ecuador, and, for several years, the Westwood city hall.

August 30, 1949, the Hudson Oil Company, 4724 Rainbow Blvd., presented an application for rezoning the area from Residential use to Retail Business. The legal description: East 1/2 of Lot 5 except the East 140 1/2 thereof in Homesland an addition in Johnson County, Kansas. The usage to be a service station. The request was denied.

Later a request was made to obtain a building permit for an office building. This request was granted. It became the home of Hudson Oil Company and an International Affairs—serving companies transactions in 32 states and also the Consular office of the Consuls for Columbia and Ecuador.

It is here Mary Hudson Vandergrift Co., the founder of Hudson Oil Company, and her husband, Frank Vandergrift (now deceased), looked after the interests of the citizens of the countries which they represented.

CURRENT WESTWOOD ATTRIBUTES

Shopping Centers enjoyed and conveniently used are:
Country Club Plaza, Mission Shopping Center, Metcalf Shopping Center, Prairie Village Shopping Center, Ward Parkway Shopping Center, and Westwood Village Shopping Center.

Outdoor recreational activities:
Citizens of Westwood use Woodside Racquet Club's swimming pools for a nominal fee, outdoor tennis courts by registering with the city and the city's own park located at 50th and Rainbow.

Schools:
Westwood View Elementary School - 2511 W. 50th Street; Shawnee Mission Christian School - 4901 Mission Road. The following schools are not located in the City of Westwood but are with in the area: St. Agnes Parochial Elementary - Mission Road at 53rd Street; Bishop Miege High School - Reinhardt; Indian Hills Junior High - 64th and Mission Road; Shawnee Mission East High School - 75th and Mission Road; Shawnee Mission North High School - Metcalf and Johnson Drive; Pembroke Day School - Shawnee Mission Parkway and State Line Road.

Churches:

Westwood Christian Church - 5050 Rainbow; Olivet Baptist Church - 4901 Mission Road; Youth for Christ - 4700 Rainbow; Westwood Lutheran Church - 5035 Rainbow; St. Agnes - 53rd and Mission Road; Old Mission United Methodist - Shawnee Mission Parkway and State Park

Radio Station:

Entercom Broadcasting - Belinder and 50th Street (AM - WDAF, KMBZ, and KCMO; FM - KUDL, KYYS, KCMO)

Parks:

Mini-Park - 50th and Rainbow (one tennis court, children's play area); two pocket/resting parks - 47th Terrace and Belinder and 47th Terrace just east of Rainbow.

Libraries:

Main Library: Johnson County (9875 West 87th Street); Cedar Roe Library

The Entercom Broadcast Center at 4935 Belinder Avenue. The twin towers of KMBZ-AM have marked Westwood's skyline for seven decades. KMBC's call letters were changed to KMBZ in 1969.

- 5120 Cedar, Roeland Park.

Water District:

Johnson County Water District #1.

Fire District:

#2 Located 63rd and Mission Road.

TERRACE GARDEN CLUB:

JAN • 60

October 1948, a group of ladies who lived northwest of Belinder organized a Garden Club and were Federated in 1951. Their meetings were held the second Thursday of each month, in their homes.

Their Motto:

The heart is a garden
Where thought flowers grow;
The thoughts that we think
Are the seeds that we sow.

Help us oh Lord, to grasp the meaning of growing things, the mystery of opening bud and winged seed—
that we may weave it into the tissue of our faith in life eternal.
Give us wisdom to cultivate our minds as diligently as we nurture tender seedlings,
and patience to weed out envy and malice as we uproot troublesome weeds.
Teach us to seek steady root growth rather than a fleeting culture, and to cultivate those traits
which brighten under adversity with the perennial loveliness of hardy borders.
Thank God for gardens and their message, "today and ALWAYS."

Charter Roster:

Akers, Jan	Cullivan, Margaret	Levering, Lois	Morrison, Margaret
Barron, Betty	Figge, Eliner	Lundbland, Margaret	Sulley, Gwen
Cain, Helen	Gardinger, Shirley	Marmon, Ruth	Thoms, Catherine
Cox, Estelle	Kraft, Eleanor	Meitner, Barbara	Young, Betty

Their studies covered many aspects of the gardening of flowers. Programs offered Garden books to read, study of certain flowers, shrubs, and bulbs, flower arrangements, tour of neighborhood gardens and special centerpieces for the holiday seasons.

WESTWOOD'S WOMEN'S CLUB

On May 14, 1969 eight Westwood residents met with Max Fiebig, Sprint's ground Keeper, to discuss forming a Garden Club in the City of Westwood. After several meetings, the Club was officially organized in October, 1969. It was decided to meet the third Wednesday of each month at 12:30. A luncheon and program would follow. The Rose was to be the flower, the Dogwood the tree, the cardinal the bird, green the color. Among our many projects we consider these to be some four outstanding:

I. We worked with the City to help educate the Public in regard to the "Dutch Elm Disease".

II. Observing Arbor Day with the Westwood View School by giving each child an evergreen or a tree seedling to be planted.

III. To encourage beautiful yards we started the selection of "Yard of the Month".

IV. The first "Garden Club Tour" was held.

Westwood Garden Club, October 1994. Tree dedication ceremony in honor of Mary Bond, the club's first president.

V. But our most successful project has been the "Senior Citizen Christmas Luncheon". Originally it was in the Westwood Christian Church. The members of the Club did the decorations, cooked the food and served the luncheon followed by a Program. We had about 100 guests.

Westwood Garden Club at a social gathering at Jackie Bay's house, May 1994

A few years ago we voted to have the luncheon catered by the Woodside Racquet club.

VI In honor of our charter Members each year we give a prize to a student at Westwood View School for the best essay in "Environmental Issue". A prize is also given for the two best essays on "Arts and in Science".

The Club is proud to be a part of our Westwood Community.

WESTWOOD NEIGHBORHOOD ASSOCIATION

The Westwood Neighborhood Association was formed in 1987. A young man by the name of Tom Shanks, a 16 year old a resident of the city, became its president. It was created, Shanks said, to give citizens another voice in the community. He stated the new Association was not a patrol group but one which would be involved into a forum for citizens discussion of concerns and a host for such community-building events.

The first citywide event was the Oktoberfest held at the mini-park on the corner of 50th and Rainbow. Residents were so pleased at the turnout that they organized a Christmas caroling event and had a good turnout for that.

The association gives an opportunity for the people to have a different point of view from the elected officials.

Westwood representatives traveled to Topeka on March 30 to receive a resolution from Governor Mike Hayden congratulating Westwood on its 40th anniversary. The resolution was sponsored by Representative Al Lane and Senator Audrey Langworthy in celebration of Westwood's anniversary

Association Plays a Major Role

The Westwood Neighborhood Association was formed two years ago by a group of interested residents. Some of the organization's objectives include encouraging maintenance and improvement of property, assisting senior citizens, and building a sense of identity and pride in the neighborhood.

In the two years of its existence the Westwood Neighborhood Association has published a service list, written and developed a grievance procedure, organized an open forum for residents to question the construction of a new city hall, and provided speakers on such timely topics as lawn care and the effect of county appraisals.

Some of the projects currently supported by the association include the beautification and establishment of city – in parks, recycling, a new resident introduction, and the 40th birthday celebration.

This is a voluntary nonpartisan organization that boasts 10 percent of the city's residents in its membership. The recruitment and renewal drive for this organization is now underway. Residents and businesses of Westwood are invited and encouraged to join.

FOUNDATION PROMOTES CITY

The Westwood Foundation is a not-for-profit organization whose original purpose was to develop the Woodside Racquet Club and the Westwood Plaza Tower office building. The Foundation exists for the benefit of residents of the city, and to promote the well being of the community.

By charter, the Mayor is the chairman of the Foundation. Residents are appointed to serve on the Board of Directors. This year Westwood Foundation sponsored the second annual $4,000 merit scholarship program for Westwood families. It also sponsored the Kansas City Chamber Orchestra, a 40th anniversary event.

City of
Westwood

**The Governing Body of the
City of Westwood, Kansas
requests the pleasure of your company
at the dedication ceremonies
and formal opening of the city's
new municipal building and city hall
Saturday, May 18, 1991
11:00 A.M.
47th and Rainbow Blvd.   Westwood, Kansas 66205
Barbeque lunch following ceremony**

WOODSIDE RACQUET CLUB

On May 1, 1986, the thought of losing Woodside Racquet Club was expressed. The management group operating the Club offered $1.8 million to the City of Westwood. The council, after much study, decided it best to keep the club according to the figures presented at their work session. The city had about $500,000 invested in the 12 acres site at 47th Place and Rainbow and stands to gain about $250,000 annually from the club once the industrial revenue bonds are paid off in the 1990's.

The city originally bought the property to control the development. Bonds were issued later to finance the ailing club when foreclosure was threatened in the 1970s.

Mr. Norman Gaar, attorney for the Westwood Foundation, stated this was done to get control of the property.

July, 1993, a grant of $63,000 was received by the council for the purpose of meeting the requirements of the Americans with Disability Act requiring all public facilities be accessible to handicapped.

The complex consists of 4 swimming pools located at the private Racquet Club, 2000 W. 47th Place. The City retains swimming and tennis privileges for the residents at the club.

The proceeds of $63,000 was a community block development fund to cover proposed modifications of the pools' bath house and the two lower-level pools. The grant had been applied for by the city through the Johnson County Small Cities Program.

John Sullivan, Public Works Director, said, "The swimming pool falls under the guide line of building covered by ADA."

Woodside Racqet Club
Aerial View
1990

Another view of the expansive Woodside Racquet Club as shown in this aerial photograph.

WESTWOOD FOUNDATION SCHOLARSHIPS

The Westwood Foundation Scholarships program was established in 1988 to recognize and reward the academics and personal achievements of younger citizens and to promote and foster personal and intellectual growth within our community.

In addition to academics accomplishments, consideration is given to extracurricular school activities and involvement in nonacademic participation such as community or charitable involvement and volunteer experience.

To be eligible, a student must be going to a vocational/technical school in the coming year and must be a Westwood resident.

A scholarship in the amount of $1,000 for each undergraduate year have been awarded to the following students:

Posing with scholarship recipient Todd E. Schulkin (center) are John Bird, Bonnie Schulkin, Mayor Bill Kostar, and Carl Schulkin.

1988	Jennifer Blackwell	Bishop Miege
1989	Todd Schulkin	Pembroke Hill
1990	Jennifer Johnson	Shawnee Mission North
1991	Shannon Martin	Shawnee Mission North
1992	Arnica Baldwin	Bishop Miege
	Jennifer Wishman	Bishop Miege
1993	Jason Elk	Shawnee Mission East
1994	Sarah Mann	Shawnee Mission North
1995	Suzanne Decker	Bishop Miege
1996	Amanda Moorhouse	Shawnee Mission East
1997	Megan Kean	Bishop Miege
1998	Annie Sutera	Bishop Miege
1999	Brett Okken	Christian Academy
	Luke Wetzel	Shawnee Mission East

Shown with Mayor Kostar are Brett Okken (left) and Luke Wetzel (right).

16

Education
Our Past & Present

A NOTE FROM THE LEEPER'S SUNSHINE SCHOOL DAY CARE

Our family chose "Westport Annex" for our home because of the Westwood View School. A professional educator recommended the district because Westwood View School's education seemed to be the top priority for our children. It proved to be the best move we could have made.

Our family attended Westwood Christian Church where I was a teacher with Dorothy Stores of the youngest Sunday School Class. From this evolved caring for the Christian Womens Fellowship children. Before long, Nadine Oatman and I were providing services for the children of the very few working mothers.

Eventually the word "Pre-School" came into play. From there we became a Pre-School Day Care. Later our daughter joined me and we became a Montessori Day Care as we remained for approximately 20 years.

We closed the School in 1989 with 40 years of child care behind us.

WESTWOOD VIEW SCHOOL

The first school in our area was at the Indian Mission. It was built by a local resident, Miles Standish. It was Shawnee Mission District No. 92. The first school district Meetings were held in the old Mission Chapel Room on August 22, 1873. The officer were: A.M. Johnson, clerk, J.E. Bernard, Treasurer, M. Greene, Director. The board members were: Miles Standish, J.C. Martin, John Swatzell, Sr., Phillip Reinhardt and John Roe. In 1875 the enrollment was 51 pupils.

During this time parents around the Westport Annex felt the distance was too far for the smaller children to walk to school. Mrs. Richard Ketrow from the annex decided to do something about it. She rode the (train) called the "Strang Line" to OLATHE, Kansas the county seat office to find the necessary steps to be taken to divided the district. A petition was circulated on August 5, 1912 and the division was finally made, territory east of the line halfway between Mission Road and Belinder was formed into School District no 93 and called Hudson School.

The Strang Line Trolley

The Strang Line Trolley ran from May 20, 1906 until August 10, 1940, carrying passengers from Westport to Olathe through areas which are now known as Roeland Park, Overland Park, and Lenexa. The first cars were gasoline powered electric engines, the first of their kind ever built. In 1908, the line converted to the electric trolley as shown here. The people catcher on the front was made of bed springs and was lowered for city travel, to keep people from falling under the wheels. —*Shirley Stiles*

The question came up where would the children go to school while the new school was being built? At this time a two story house was just built on Hamilton street (now 48th Street) and arrangements were made for the children to use it for the school.

A two room brick building was built on 48th. Street west of Hudson Road (now Rainbow Blvd.). Later a room was built in the basement for the primary pupils while the intermediate and upper grades used the original rooms. Later a two room frame building was built east of the brick building to take care of the increasing number of school children. The school became a very popular place. It was a community meeting place and many interesting programs were held there. Teachers from Kansas University came and gave extension classes in painting, interior decorating and sewing.

Hudson School, 1912-1928

Due to the growth of the enrollment there was a discussion to move to the south and build a new school. Those that had worked hard to get the Hudson School didn't want to make the move again for again they it was too far for the younger children. After several meetings a vote was taken and by a simple majority the move was authorized. Mr. M. M. Rivard a resident of Westwood Hills was a school board member and made the statement about the discussion "The static in the air would light a match." He told of the board buying a cow and the board members would take turn to milk the cow and deliver milk to some of the children homes in order for them to have milk to drink. In January, 1928 the school site was changed to 50th Street west of Rainbow Blvd. and renamed Westwood View School Number 93 and a new building. When the old Hudson was demolished the lumber from the wooden building adjacent to the brick building was used to construct two homes on that site. The early Hudson principals were Lillian Payne, Miss Boles and Harry Cyrtis.

WESTWOOD VIEW SCHOOL
1928 - 1969

20

The land for the new school was purchased from the Swatzell Family. The family owned 380 acres of the land in what is now Westwood and Westwood Hills through the original land grant to the Shawnee Indians by their one-time chief Captain Joseph Parks. What is now Westwood Hills was once the dairy farm for one of the Swatzell brothers. The stone house on the Northwest corner of 50th and Rainbow was and still owned by the Swatzell Family.

In September, 1931 C.A. "Pete" Fordyce came to Westwood View as the Principal.

During Mr. Fordyce's term as principal the school grew in attendance and many programs were established. They also enjoyed the inheritance of a collection of models which are on display in the school library. They include sailing ships, a covered wagon, a stage coach antique farm implements, an oil derrick, mining shack, spinning wheel, Dutch windmill, Indian teepee, colonial house, and a Swedish house were the products of a Federal Government Project during the Depression Era of the 1930's.

In 1935 the enrollment was 216 students and by 1946 it had grown to 309.

During the World war II in November the school collected 23,730 pounds of paper. With the proceeds war bonds were purchased.

A boy and girls basket ball teams had been organized and they played in tournaments.

Enrollment continued to grow and new classrooms were added to the new school. Five new rooms added to the south or back side of the school. At the same time additional grounds were added to include a playground for the lower grades. Even the faculty had grown in number of 17 in 1945-46.

"Pete" Fordyce

In 1947 Mr. Fordyce resigned as principal to take a job with A.S. Weltner Investment Company of Kansas City, Missouri. He had served as principal for 16 years and had quietly and privately helped many of his students through troublesome times. It was hard to give it up. But he lived only four years after his retirement. He died October 23, 1951.

His successor was Mr. Wylie V. Harris. Mr. Harris came from the administrative position in a Topeka System.

New methods were introduced in the teaching areas. New subject were introduced as: Typing, Spanish language, Physical Education classes added for both girls and boys. Many things were unique in Westwood View. The teacher were given freedom to try new ideas an example in one class room it contained desks painted such colors as red, blue, lavender, green and orange. Mr. Basel (teacher) remembers that one student had a lavender desk, lavender coat, and a lavender Kleenex box.

Mr. Harris key word was "individual" He felt Education had traditionally treated children as member of pre-established grade groups and each grade has followed a pre-determined course of study with little consideration given to him as a individual person.

Wylie V. Harris

Other groups were introduced for language arts. Mathematics, Science, Social Studies. Even different grade level were put together of those interested in such subject. Groups of all boys and all girls were tried for a short period. The two groups were tried for two years but for lack of willing new participants it was not continued.

21

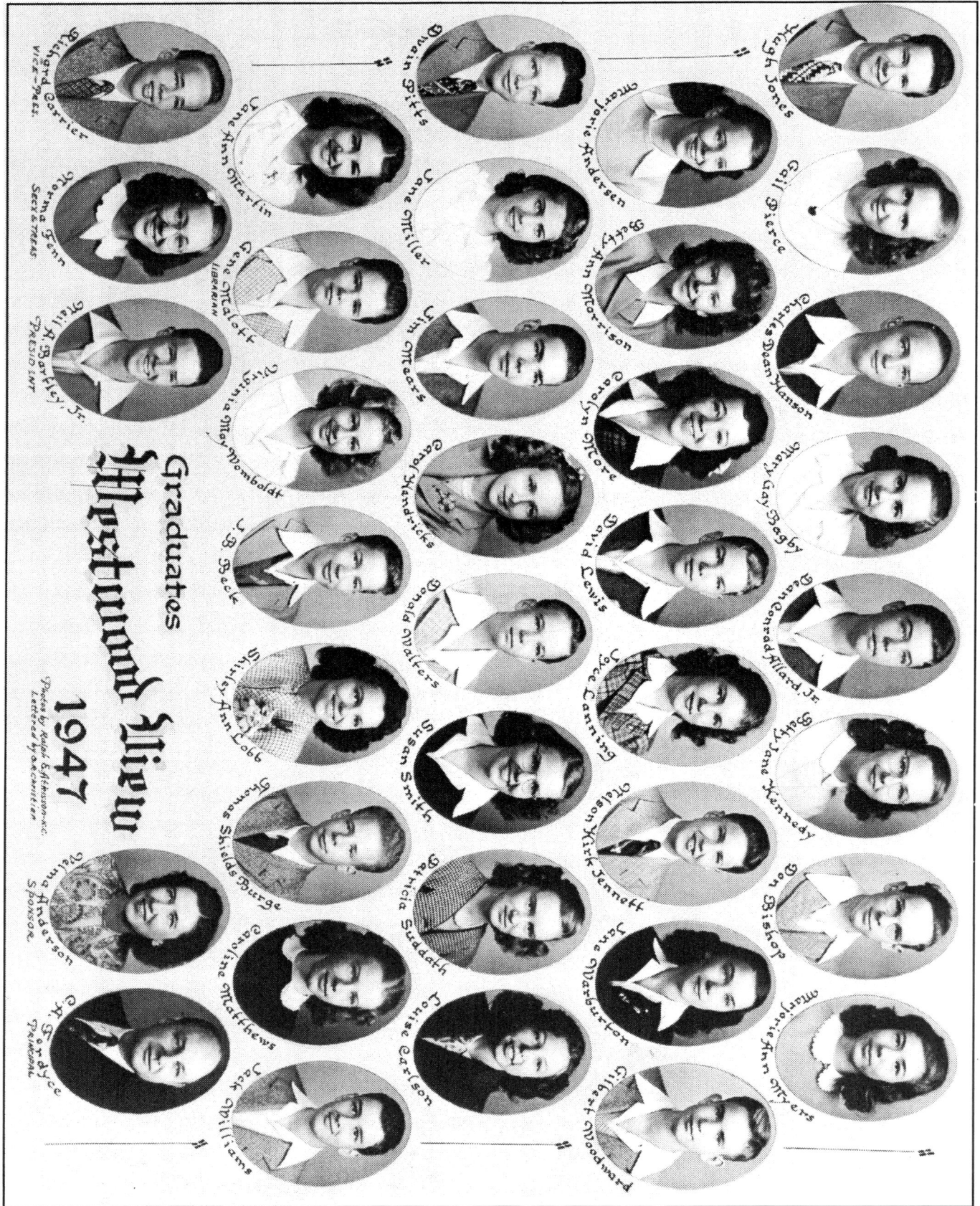

Graduates

Westwood View

1947

Richard Carrier — Vice-Pres.
Norma Fenn — Sec & Treas.
R. Bartley, Jr. — President

Velma Anderson — Sponsor
C.A. Gordyce — Principal

Jane Ann Martin
June Malott — Librarian
Victoria May Wombolt
L.B. Beck
Shirley Ann Lobb
Thomas Shields Burge
Caroline Matthews
Jack Williams

Jane Miller
Jim Mears
Carol Hendricks
Donald Walters
Susan Smith
Patricia Suddath
Lenore Carlson
Gilbert Woodward

Dwain Sitts
Betty Ann Morrison
Carolyn Moore
David Lewis
Joyce Canning
Nelson Kirk Jennett
Jane Warburton

Marjorie Andersen
Hugh Jones
Gail Pierce
Charles Dean Hanson
Mary Gay Bagby
Dean Conrad Allard, Jr.
Betty Jane Kennedy
Don Bishop
Marjorie Ann Myers

Board of Education

V. E. Reames
R. W. Speer
R. B. Rose

———

Dorothy DeVault, County Supt.

———

Faculty

Charles A. Fordyce

Jane Dean Riggs

Opal A. Smith

Orpha E. Jones

Bonnie L. Wallace

Jewell M. Quick

Velma Anderson

Louise McKinney

Graduating Exercises

Westwood View School

MONDAY EVENING

EIGHT O'CLOCK

MAY TWENTY-FIRST
NINETEEN HUNDRED THIRTY-FOUR

Processional ....Miss Velma Anderson

Invocation ....Rev. R. C. Harding

Salutatory ....Victor White

Class History ....Nelson Hunter

Piano Solo ....Ruth Quick

Class Will ....Betty Lou Wisner

Reading ....Juanita Burns

Vocal Solo ....Miss Velma Anderson

Address ....Rev. Roy Zimmer

Class Song

Valedictory ....Kathryn McClellan

Presentation of Diplomas ....Dorothy DeVault
Co. Supt. of Schools

Benediction

GRADUATES

———

Juanita Burns

Laura May Childers

Margaret Childers

James Hammons

Nelson Hunter

Wilma Massey

Kathryn McClellan

Anna Metzler

Ruth Quick

Pauline Stevens

Victor White

Betty Lou Wisner

———

Class Motto — Not Finished, just begun.
Class Flower — Rose.
Class Colors — Peach and Silver.

There was question if was the proper way to teach but the success of the academic programs at Westwood View was proven by a survey in 1960 of the students who had entered kindergarten in 1947 and graduated from either Shawnee Mission North or East in 1960. Forty-eight boys and girls that had started in Westwood View and thirty-three still lived in the are graduated in 1960. Three-fourth of these students were considered honor academic students maintaining an A or B average. Five of them ranked in the top one-half of one percent on the National Merit Scholarship Test. One was valedictorian and one was salutatorian of his or her class.

Bottom row: Miss Shay, Miss Green, Miss Newland, Miss McFadden, Miss Fredericks. Middle row: Miss Auy, Miss Glenn, Wiss Wallace, Miss McDonald, Miss Anderson, Mr. Fordyce. Back Row: Miss Wittsett, Miss Babb, Miss Fisher, Miss Riggs, Miss Goebel.

Music was established in 1940 and continued through 1970, the class met every day. Private instrumental instructors came to the school to give students private lesson , which were arranged so no class work was missed. The private lessons were paid for by the parents.

Square dancing was a part of the regular music program, meeting once a month. At various times there was a girls and boys chorus and a harmonica choir. Christmas was an important time at Westwood View. Mr. Keller of the Rainbow Nursery donated a live Christmas tree for each classroom and a very large tree was located in the front hall. At least a week before Christmas the children gathered around the tree in the morning to sing Christmas carols. People from the community often came to listen. The Christmas pageant performed for the parents was known as the "Living Christmas Carols".

Art as a Specialty was slower to develop than music and physical education. But the teacher of first and second grades was interested in art and through her art began to increase. She was involved in developing the exhibits which later formed the traveling exhibits of Hallmarks' Kaleidoscope. Today Rachel Chambers is the Director of Kaleidoscope, and she reports that between 500,000 and 600,000 children had now enjoyed the program, a program born at Westwood View School

Westwood View School, 3rd & 4th grades, circa September, 1930
Teacher, Mrs Scott
Front row: Gladys Peterson, Grace Quick, Margaret Peterson, __ Turley, Margaret Ann Lehrack, ?, Emily Ann Mullins, ?
Second row: ?, David Hammons, Phillip Hedman, Bobby Adams, Paul Turner Donald Parr, Junior Harris, Park Worrel.
Third row: Geneva Allen, Marjorie Thies, ?, ?, ?, ?, Leroy Ives, ?, Edward Schulteis.
Back Row: Kenneth Glayzer, ?, Reinhold Schreiner, Jack Morrison, Irene Turley, ?, ?, Clarra Wombolt, Pearl Wise

Mr. Wylie Harris resigned his position as principal and left Westwood View in June 1966. He had been with the school for 19 years. In tribute to Mr. Harris he as presented with an expression of appreciation and esteem by the members of the Board of Education. This expression described him as the "educational architect and chief administrator of Westwood View School District No 93.

We must give credit to the many teachers who dedicated a portion of their lives to our students.

Unification was to bring another change in the life of Westwood View School. The Shawnee Mission District introduced Unification and the Westwood residents of our District was against the new program. A vote was taken and rejected by 5,733 to 2,954. But the rapid development of Unification through the State made Northeast Johnson County unification inevitable. A special Act by Kansas Legislature passes February 13, 1969, signed by Governor Robert Docking that No. 93 was dissolved and Westwood View became Building Number 101 of the Unified District.

A bond election was held January 19, 1965 for purpose to build a new unit to the existing structure and renovated the present building. This bond issue failed.

Dedication

WESTWOOD VIEW SCHOOL

MAY 4, 1969

**WESTWOOD VIEW SCHOOL DISTRICT
JOHNSON COUNTY, KANSAS**

A new superintendent was employed in July 1966 and he worked diligently for the construction of the new building. He was Dr. William R. Foster who came to Westwood View from Fargo, North Dakota. After Don Farmer, Mr. Dana Basel became the principal. The school board didn't give up and another election was held on September 23, 1967 and the issue passed. The bonds were sold at a public sealed bid. They were dated March 1, 1968 and last one matured in 1988. The new building started shortly after the bond issue passed. When the new building was completed, the old one was demolished. At the dedication program the new building was described "The school is a unique pod arrangement which allowed considerable saving with less hall space." The construction of the new building was controversial and the controversy still surface with patrons who had associations with the old Westwood View Building. But the fact remains that today the students at Westwood View attend school in a modern building built by the patrons off the school community.

By the beginning school year September 1969 Westwood View District No 93 ceased to exist. Shawnee Mission Unified School District 512 came into existence and Dr. William R. Foster had left to take a position at East Area District as Superintendent.

Westwood View had a brand new building , a new principal and was governed by a Unified School District. A new chapter was to begin.

Another chapter entered into Westwood View. The Unified District had a long range study made by Cresap, McCormick and Paget Inc. to conduct a study of school facilities. Their recommendation was the closing of six elementary school in 1981-1982 school year. This was quite a shock to the patrons of the school. Donna Muiller the PTA president notified parents of the happenings. A committee was formed. Al Ticwart and Scott Gard became co-chairman and took over. During the summer of 1980 volunteers conducted a census of the entire area. They covered 1,225 homes and had response from 1,120.What made this group so masterful was asked. First they were positive, had the sense of purpose that the school is important, the area is diverse, and lastly speed was important for within two weeks of the release of the report the group had formed 10 committees and gather data to refute the report. The doors remained opened. A GREAT DAY.

Through other Principals the Westwood View School has seen other changes and continue to grow in the needs of our children in this area. The PTA continues very strong in all of their activities and volunteer work. May it always be that way.

Westwood View would not be the same for one person who devoted several years of his life to take care of the building and the upkeep. That man was Mr. Elmer Laiord the custodian, a job he handled for 23 years. He started in 1935 and continued until 1958 when he retired due to ill health. He was the whole maintenance crew. During the summer month he worked preparing the inside for a perfect spotless school. You dare not step on the gymnasium floor with street shoes or you were in trouble. That was a no-no. (He always said "No, no, no. Not with your street shoes.")

MY MEMORIES OF WESTWOOD AND WESTWOOD VIEW SCHOOL
By April Keller Burger

My memories of Westwood bring a smile to my face. In Westwood, growing up, was a carefree feeling. You could walk or bike the entire city on sidewalks, and not be afraid or worried. Neighbors waved, you could walk up to strangers. Westwood was a secure, friendly city.

Trick-or-treating at Halloween in the 1960s was totally safe. A group of us kids would walk the city with our pillowcases, trick-or-treating, and be out until 8:30 P.M.. There was no need for an adult to go along. When I take my daughter trick-or-treating now, I drive her only to those houses of folks I know.

In Westwood, neighbors trusted neighbors. For example, there was a minimal chain fence around my parent's Garden Center, Rainbow Nursery. There was practically nothing stopping someone who was dishonest, but the wonderful thing about it was the trust that they had for mankind.

We walked to school every day. At lunch time we walked home. Sometimes after school, we'd walk to Fairway to the Bogdon's Candy Store and get some mints or reception sticks. When we got older, we went to Dari-O (Regan's bought it) or Allen's Drive-In. At Allen's you could sit in a booth for lunch, and select your favorite song to play on the jukebox. Only 5 cents each or 5 for 25 cents.

The only school I know was the old Westwood View. I attended Westwood View School from 1959 to 1967. I loved all my teachers and the principal, Wylie V. Harris.

The floor plan, in the book Westwood View School; Seventy-Two Years Plus by Karen J. Johnson, September, 1984 on page 20, is not how I remember the layout of Westwood View. As in most floor plans, it was not uncommon for plans to change.

Kindergarten was held where the music room is shown. The music room was on the opposite side of the building, where the second grade is shown, nearest the girl's bathroom. Typing was held on the stage. In the typing room on the floor plan, was a fifth grade class, taught by Mr. Edward Plumb and later Mr. Fuqua. I have many memories of my school days at Westwood, from my kindergarten class, when I had what is called today "team teaching" with a teacher from

England, Miss Garside, and with my regular teacher, Miss Shay, up to sixth grade, with Geraldine Kinkaid as my teacher.

Passing through the halls, on my left and right, were huge class pictures of past graduates of Westwood View. It was always fun to look at them. My older brother's pictures was in one of the frames that I could admire. It was a big honor to have your class picture displayed in the hallways. I was anxiously awaiting the time that I would see my class picture there.

On the left hand side of the school, just past the second grade rooms, there was an ice cream machine. It was in the hallway just before the door to the outside. The machine held fudge bars, Eskimo pies and ice cream sandwiches. There were also a few lockers in that hallway.

As you climbed the stairs to the second floor, straight ahead, in front of the balcony, was a long set of glass cases that enclosed models of dinosaurs and ships and dolls. These cases ran the entire length of the upstairs balcony.

We would go out on the playground, we had a big blacktop area. The girls would pick teams and play kickball. Sometimes we played 4-square. I don't know what the boys were playing. We also had various playground equipment.

One of my girlfriends' father would come to school once in a while. He always would have candy when he came to school. He came out to the playground and shared it. His daughter's name was Vida Bikales.

I walked to school. I took several "routes," sometimes alone, and sometimes I "picked up" my friends who lived along the way. They were happy times. I was never afraid to walk to or from school alone. Westwood was a very **safe** place to live, work and go to school.

Westwood View was a very **progressive** school. School officials had a vision. Students had the opportunity of learning a second language, Spanish, with Miss Chavez, from

April Keller Burger

the first grade and also typing, with Mrs. Helen Adams, during grades 5 and 6. I've appreciated many times throughout my years, the advancement that those two subjects gave me over other elementary students. After having my own family, I realize that Westwood View was way before its time, as even 30 some years later, schools have yet to follow its lead in progressiveness.

Another indication of progressiveness was in individualized education. When I was in third grade, my teacher, **Irene Mitchell**, recognized that I loved spelling. In third grade I began at that level of spelling, and by the end of the year I had moved up 4 entire grades, completing the 7th grade speller.

While I attended Westwood View, grades were sometimes combined. In 4th grade there were 3rd and 4th graders. In second grade were 1st and 2nd. What was really great was that I had my 1st and 2nd teacher two years in a row and my 3rd and 4th grade teacher was the same. I think this gave students and teachers a unique advantage. The student would get to know the teacher and her style of teaching, and learning would flow smoothly from one year to the next. The teacher also got to know the student and his style of learning and would be able to work more closely with the student. This plan worked for me.

Westwood View teachers were unique. They had many new ideas for teaching. They wanted parental involvement, but also realized that a family has boundaries. When I was in 5th grade, my teacher, **Verle Krehbiel** scheduled my grade card conference at my house. Both of my parents worked in the family business, and he was kind enough to work around our family schedule.

I remember, in third or fourth grade, the hubbub when **Miss Chambers** (the art teacher who also taught third and fourth grade) was in the very early stages of what would become Hallmark's "Kaleidoscope," and how the children of Westwood were her first "subjects." How impressive.

Miss Anderson used to read us stories. That was a

27

very special time. She kept everything just so, in the library. We had an immense selection of the most wonderful books. I remember that in the library was a huge, comfortable living room type chair to the left, in the corner, that we were allowed to sit in and read. Or course, we had to take turns, but sometimes you could get two or three people in it. If a student read a certain number of books, he was eligible for a William Allen White Award from the University of Kansas in recognition of this accomplishment. Almost opposite the door to the library, in the far left corner, bracketed to the wall was the TV. It may have been black and white. I only remember the television being on once. I also remember distinctly that I was in Miss Anderson's library when the news came that President Kennedy was shot.

Mr. Harris was a marvelous principal. He was so knowledgeable. I remember his coming into my sixth grade in Geraldine Kinkaid's class and talking about one of his trips to Tanzania. You could almost picture the country when he talked about it. He made a point to get to know each child's name in the entire school. Mr. Harris taught us that the difference between "principle" and "principal" is that a "principal" is your pal. Some of the boys got to know him better, because they had to go to the office. Those were the days when a principal could actually punish a student physically.

The typing class was held on the stage. We had typing class alternating with Spanish. Mrs. **Helen Adams** was the typing teacher. Westwood View was very innovative and until joining the "unified school district," was probably the only grade school in the area that offered typing and Spanish. The fact that I had typing in grade school helped me tremendously in my school years, and in dealing with the computer age.

The most wonderful time of the year was Christmas. The school was beautifully decorated, with a Christmas tree in every single classroom. Then Westwood View had a total of 14 classrooms, plus there was a tree in the office and in the gym/auditorium. My parents, **George and Marie Keller**, owned Rainbow Nursery Garden Center, at 4740 Rainbow and donated trees to the school each year for 10 years. This type of generosity was prevalent among Westwood residents. We were a family. When Rainbow Nursery closed its doors, the Nursery donated to the school its artificial trees.

Mrs. Lashbrook was the music teacher. She was also in charge of the **Christmas Program**. Mrs. Lashbrook and Miss Anderson worked tirelessly to put on a beautiful show. Mrs. Lashbrook was in charge of the vocal music and Miss Anderson played the piano. We had the same play year after year, but somehow it was always "new." The play was always held in the auditorium/gymnasium. The sixth graders were featured in the play, trying out for major parts such as narrator, three wise men, Mary and Joseph. During the play, there was a scene in which someone was carrying a load of yule logs across the stage on a sleigh. There was a lot of competition to get the part of the person riding the yule logs. The fifth and sixth grades had the honor of singing from the balcony which overlooked the gym. "On Holy Night" was one of the songs we sang, one of my favorites. It was sung by the 5th and 6th graders, above the gym, in the balcony. Only 5th and 6th graders could sit in the balcony. And just before the song created to the phrase, "fall, on your knees," the kids in the balcony would rise, which gave a beautiful emphasis to the emotional song.

Mrs. Lashbrook always had trouble with those of us who, instead of "westward leading" insisted on singing "Westwood leading, still proceeding, guide us to thy perfect light." I guess we just couldn't help it. As upperclassmen, we sere **so** proud of Westwood View and the solid background it gave us.

This particular program was held in the new school. Miss Anderson played the piano in one corner, and I played the organ in the opposite corner. I'm not sure if this is the "original" program that I remember, but I do know that she divided the singing groups differently, since the new school did not have a balcony for the 5th and 6th grade.

My mother, **Marie Keller**, was a room mother for many years, as there were four Keller children attending Westwood View. One Halloween she dressed up like a witch for the school party, with the ugliest and biggest wart on her nose. When she walked in to the door of the school, the principal, Wylie Harris said, "Hello, Mrs. Keller." I guess her wart wasn't big enough after all!!!

During a tornado drill at the new school, my dad, **George Keller**, was at the time the Chief of Civil Defense. He clearly remembers standing at the steps of Westwood View and seeing a tornado loom extremely close to the City of Westwood. The children were sitting in the hallways with their heads down already, and there was nothing to do but watch. My father was prepared to give his life, serving his civil duty, along with all those school children. Thankfully, the tornado did not touch down in Westwood.

I continue to have special feelings for the City of Westwood and Westwood View School. I'm proud to say that I grew up in such a wonderful city.

From: Susan Wrightsman Swanson

A description of the layout of Westwood View School by former student Susan Wrightsman Swanson who grew up living at 2509 W. 50th. Place with her parents.

Walk through the front door turn to the right. Walk to the wall. I was in first and second grade in this room. Miss Coleman was my teacher. The hall turns left. At the end of the hall, if you turn left you go into the gym. If you slightly turn right, then a quick jog to the left, there is the girls bathroom on the right, Boys on the left. The next room after the bathroom is Mrs. Lashbrook's classroom (music room). The room at the end of the hall on the right was my 3rd grade room with Miss Burchfield/Mrs. Norton back up the hall, going by the girls bathroom a quick look to the left is a double door going outside to the playground.

There is also a single door by my 3rd grade room and it lets you out by the stairs that reach the roof!! (also, by the "4-square" Game)!! Anyway, turn right at the end of the hall and on your left is the secretary's office. Mr., Harris (Principal) office was to the back of that, then it was the nurse's office. To the left and back was the huge staircase up to the library and the upper grade classes. 5th and 6th grades go to the end of the hall; turn right, and on the left is my 4th grade classroom with Mrs. Mitchell. The hall jogs again to the left, a quick right passing the girls bathroom and the kindergarten room should be on the right at the end of the hall turn around and go back up the hall and the double doors are now to your right. Do remember there were some lockers there? And the drive where our moms could pick up in nasty weather? Faye Catlette flushed my slip down the toilet one time in fourth grade. She was such a mean little _____ always calling "war" on one of us and making is all hate each other until she decided we could all be friends but only for a few days. Then it was someone else's turn.

The janitor always let us watch "Price is Right" during lunch. Diane Diedrich use to gross me out when she would bring sardine sandwiches YUCK. Don't know the nurse or the secretary name never must have had to go there. The art room was behind the stage in the gym and the typing room was on the stage. The art teacher was Miss Caldwell I think, and I remember when Hal Wenzel dripped paint on my picture and he and I had to write something 500 times because I got all upset and she thought we were goofing off.

I do remember the ice cream machine in the same hallway downstairs as the lockers, but seems to me could only get it once a week...or maybe that's the only time mom gave a dime!!!

I remember two incidences with Greg. Once we had a tornado drill and he was in the boys bathroom n the west side of the gym our classroom was to go to the boys bathroom to duck and there he was (the clown!!) acting like he was using one of those sideways bathtubs that the boys use. He really wasn't but he had planned to make it look like he was!! The other time in 6th grade he was in Mr. Basil's class jumping and trying to reach the flag right by the door. He was so intent and really concentrating on just being able to touch it, Mr. Basil snuck up behind him and paddled him. Poor Greg. Mr. Basil was good to David though. I remember going with your mom to take David to Mr. Basil's for summer tutoring

For me the fifth and sixth grades were on the left and right upstairs. I'm sure this changed yearly as age enrollment changed.

"We said the pledge of allegiance at the beginning of every day each classroom had a flag." (April Keller Burger's quote).

Mayors' Memories

William Weeks

I bought my house in Westwood in 1950 and lived there 10 years. We had 10 wonderful years there with many fond memories.

I had my first taste of politics running for council and a short time as Mayor.

William Weeks

This was during the time of a strained budget and a bad city image of writing tickets to make the budget (this was before Hallmark and Sprint). The *Kansas City Star* wrote some articles about our city and its Gestapo Police Department, that were anything but true. It took a while but we finally convinced the paper to get rid of their man who covered our city and monthly meetings and assign someone who would tell the truth.

Being mayor of a small city has its advantages and disadvantages, including some of the calls you would get, such as barking dogs, people burning leaves smoking up the neighbor's laundry, chuck holes, etc. It was a great experience that I will always remember and cherish forever. It was a great honor to serve a great city.

Thanks.

William "Bill" Weeks

Norman E. Gaar

I am happy to write this letter to you for the possible use of excerpts of it to celebrate the 50th year of the municipal birth of the City of Westwood, Kansas. It is written in a rather disjointed, free association style because I neglected to keep a diary of the many events which occurred and the various circumstances in which I found myself during the years I worked for and lived in Westwood.

Norman E. Gaar

In 1956, after battling my way through college, the Korean War, and law school, I returned to Johnson County, the home of my youth. I decided that I did not want to live in south Johnson County (that is, any place north of 75th Street), and all I could remember about the Westwood of my youth was the large open field with a radio tower in its center. It was my good fortune, however, to find a small house for sale directly across from that large field with its big tower, and I moved into it in 1957. The dance had begun.

I soon learned that Westwood city government was in a state of turmoil, and I decided to figure out how I could help. One evening while walking north on Mission Road I heard a loud "flap, flap, flap" behind me and I turned around to see a police cruiser slowly stop beside me. An officer leaned out the window and asked me what my business was. That was a fateful meeting because the cruiser was driven by a Police Officer named Mooney. After a little bit of conversation, he admitted that the flapping noise was the retread pulling away from the police cruiser's tire.

Officer Mooney suggested to this newly minted Westwood resident that something needed to be done about the city government and the ability of the Westwood Police Department to function properly. After a series of adventures, I ran for and was twice elected as the Westwood municipal judge and once as Mayor, running against and beating Officer, then "candidate," Mooney who no longer approved of my civic endeavors.

At that time Westwood had a reputation as a speed trap with a dangerous police court and this young lawyer, fresh out of law school, was determined to change that image. I was determined to reorganize the court and make it a model of American Bar Association standards. It was a bit difficult to accomplish that task.

The Municipal Court was located just east of 47th and Mission Road in a little wooden building situated on the edge of a graveled parking lot (and Westwood's method of detecting speeding drivers was not much more sophisticated.) Westwood's finest stretched two timer hoses across the suspect street at a measured distance apart. The impact of the car's tires on the first hose would trigger an impulse that initiated the timing. When the tires of the automobile impacted the second hose, the timing was converted into miles per hour and the officer would read the gage and, on a good day, issue a speeding ticket. This was not exactly rocket science technology, but it worked and a number of suspects, ticket in hand, walked into my court.

The Court frequently worked late into the evening. One such evening brought this new law school graduate and municipal judge a most perplexing female defendant. She was the wife of the City Attorney John Keach and the mother of my former Prairie School classmate, John Eulich. Sally Keach was an erudite, published author of her autobiography, *White Mother in Africa*. Needless to say, I was overly tense, Sally Keach was visibly embarrassed, and John Keach quietly sat in a corner, coolly observing the scene. I wasn't sure how to handle this, but I knew I had to play it straight and so I assumed the appropriate serious expression. Evidence was presented and no rebuttal was offered, so I fined Mrs. Keach $18. She was mortified. Then in a flash of high school brilliance, I recalled the ride of Paul Revere. I looked at her very solemnly and said, "just remember Mrs. Keach, one (timer hose) is for counting, and two is for speed" paraphrasing the Paul Revere quote, "one if by land, two if by sea". The tension between the two of us evaporated, Mrs. Keach practically collapsed in laughter, John Keach harrumped and the rest of the people in the courtroom simply sat and stared, confused in ignorance. So much for education!

On another occasion, I brought a halt to one former mayor's political favor of fixing his supporters' tickets. He was paying his supporters' traffic tickets and then calling them and telling them that he "got them off." That caper stopped when I found out about it and started mailing the citizens receipts for the fine paid to the court by the mayor to "get them off." He was simply using a non-court appearance procedure that anyone could use, except for serious traffic violations. Maybe the American Bar Association would have approved. At any rate, the court became a recognized model of procedure recommended as a visiting site to other municipal judges.

Several important land acquisitions were made by Westwood during my tenure as Mayor and shortly thereafter. In one case, the city was able to purchase the property that became the Westwood Park rather than leave it to become yet another commercial development. This purchase grew out of my friendship with Kenneth Howard, John Keacher's successor as City Attorney. Kenneth Howard was the executor of the will of the deceased owner of a ramshackle, beat up, decrepit house that sat approximately in the middle of what is now the Park. When I broached the subject with him, he agreed that the land was admirably suited to become a park and sold it to the city. I believe a portion of the property was also sold to the Westwood View Common School District. No public auction, hot shot developers, or political pressure was involved; just a fair price for an "eyesore" that was transformed into a community asset.

Joe Dennis succeeded me as Mayor, and I went on to become a member of the State Senate. Two property acquisitions made during Joe's tenure were instrumental in making Westwood a particularly attractive place to live and raise a family. The first purchase was the old Hallmark building campus located on Shawnee Mission Parkway. Joe and I were able to locate a sympathetic ear within Hallmark's management when the company relocated their offices. We were able to convince Hallmark of the merits of selling the property to a tenant appropriate to the best interests of Westwood. Any of a number of prospective buyers were turned down until a tiny little western Kansas telephone company came along. United Telephone Company was looking for a corporate headquarters, and they had an expansion-minded management. Joe and I (mostly Joe) did all we could to encourage their relocation to Westwood and the effort was successful. You know them today as Sprint. Until a year or two ago, when that company outgrew everything in sight and decided to relocate, consolidating its world headquarters in Overland Park, the Westwood taxpayer was abundantly rewarded for the efforts made to bring this little company into our community.

The other property acquisition that I remember vividly was one made through Joe Dennis' friendship with Clarence Goppert. Clarence was a banker who owned a rough, weed infested, rocky terrace of land bordered on the north by the boundary of Wyandotte and Johnson Counties and on the south, between State Line and Rainbow, by 47th Place. A group called Youth for Christ had constructed a building on the west side of the property, fronting on 47th place and

Rainbow. They were doing good things for a lot of kids, but had attracted the attention of some rather rowdy groups of youths who were ridiculing that organization's attempt to provide clean, wholesome family recreation for young people. That is, until these youths were brought into my court by the Westwood Police Chief, Al Wrinkle, who accused them of trespassing, disturbing the peace, inciting riots and dressing slovenly. My tolerance for that category of activity was low then (still is) and the problem was immediately solved with appropriate fines and weekend sentences of street storm water gutter cleaning. Yes, I made the little darlings get their hands dirty shoveling leaves and mud. And strangely enough, it cured their interest in errant activity.

Clarence Goppert decided to get rid of the remainder of the property and Joe and the council thought the city ought to buy it. We conjured up a series of steps that kept us within existing Kansas statutes and still enabled the city to acquire the property, build a tennis facility, a swimming pool, and a separate office building that survived rather turbulent years. The property now provides the funds to pay for civic projects and give scholarships to the children of Westwood residents, among other things. The means to achieving this end was the Westwood Foundation. It provides both swimming and tennis facilities for Westwood residents and social and athletic club that you are automatically eligible to join if you live in the city. It is debt free and has been used as a model community service by other municipalities.

My service in Westwood city government ended when a seat became vacant in the Kansas Senate, due to the death of a good friend and fine person, Clark Kuppinger. Since I did not know any better at the time, I thought I might be able to do some good by running for that seat, but as usual, I had to go up hill against the existing political party power structure. However, it provided no match for Joe Dennis' talents as a campaign manager. He conjured up thousands of dollars of free publicity and huge pictures in the *Kansas City Star* by staging such media events as rounding up a loose mule and having my picture taken with it, and putting me in the back seat of an open cockpit airplane to tow a banner over the district touting my election. At any rate, I won and for a short time I was the only politician in Kansas to be property addressed as Mayor and Senator at the same time.

My political opponents didn't fully appreciate what they were up against in Joe Dennis. They had not done their homework; they hadn't followed Joe's city campaigns for municipal judge and mayor. Westwood always had a rather lively municipal election, at least when it was young and rambunctious, and they learned their lesson too late to keep me out of the Senate seat.

Joe's political opponents soon developed the tactic of coming out with a last minute mayoral election eve shot at him and the group that he was leading. The first time this happened we were all greatly disturbed and were not sure how to react. However, once burned, we were ready for them the next time. Joe had access to a printing press at his office. Consequently when the expected last shot "dirt sheet" came out, liberally rearranging the facts pertaining to Joe's service in office, we were ready. We hit the basement where the printing press was located, three or four people composed, Joe set up the type, and our rebuttal went out in the hands of a small army of neighborhood children bribed with cookies and other enticing rewards. By midnight the answer in the form of a "truth sheet" was being delivered to every house in Westwood. The opposition never caught on to our rapid response technique and, consequently, the "dirt sheet" election campaign ploy collapsed. Someone told me the U.S. Defense Department was interested in interviewing Joe at the time to see if they could gain some knowledge about his talent for quick response but I never did run that rumor down, so I cannot vouch for its authenticity. Besides, the Cold War is over and we won ——————— I think!

As a mature, small Kansas municipality, Westwood has come out of its early and sometimes tumultuous birth with an amazingly large group of dedicated citizens looking out for its future. The Fitzpatrick, Jones, Dunn, Lutz, Dennis and Kostar leaders of this grand little city, along with many other Westwood citizens, have made it an icon among places to live in Kansas.

Happy Birthday to my (former) neighbors!
Very truly yours,
Norman E. Gaar

Joe Dennis

Today, we all know Westwood as a thriving, prosperous community, with fine city services and a well-staffed and well-equipped police department. But, it wasn't always that way.

When I first became Mayor of Westwood back in 1965, the city annual budget was about $60,000, hardly more than a typical household income in Westwood these days. We had only two full-time employees, a police chief and an officer who had to share a single police car, and, until we bought a surplus Army jeep and equipped it with a rinky-dink snowplow in the late 1960s, we had no maintenance equipment whatsoever.

Helping Westwood get from where it was then to where it is now has been one of the most rewarding experiences I've had in a very rewarding life. I'm proud to have played a role in our community for almost one half of its 50 year history.

Joe Dennis

My involvement with Westwood began almost by accident and my first city government post was anything but glamorous. About a year after I moved here in 1960, my neighbor, Buford Lutz, the Mayor at the time, talked me into serving on a grievance committee. We heard from people complaining about the neighbor's dog, worried about businesses moving into the area, about anything you can imagine.

Given that beginning, it's maybe surprising in retrospect that two years later, I agreed to run for municipal judge. My good friend and neighbor, and Westwood's municipal judge at that time, Norm Gaar, was running for Mayor, and he talked me into running as part of a slate we called the City Party.

My opponent was a lawyer and I wasn't, and, when we won, I was surprised and scared to death. I had no experience being a judge, but I got the hang of it, with Norm's help, and it turned out to be really fun.

Our City Hall was in the old Hudson Oil office building at 47th Terrace and Rainbow, and we had police court in the same room where we had council meetings. I handled mostly traffic cases, speeding and DWIs and I'll tell you we used to get these lead-footed kids in there every month.

I remember one kid in particular, from Mission Hills, whose dad had bought him a Corvette. He was in court all the time and I got sick of seeing him. Finally I sat down and read the statute and determined that the harshest penalty we could give this kid was a $500 fine and 30-day jail sentence. So he showed up in court with his dad and I announced the penalty and you'd have thought I'd ordered the kid hanged.

But, then I said I would suspend the penalty if he would agree to come in four Saturdays in a row and clean the streets in Westwood. We always tried to be innovative, and that became pretty standard practice in Westwood after that. Kids learned their lesson if they had to give up part of their weekends working, instead of talking their parents out of some money to pay a fine. Over the years, we put more than 600 kids, boys and girls both, through that program and I think we only had about seven repeaters.

We caught the attention of the press as well with that program. I remember one headline in particular, from the *Kansas City Times*, which read, "Blistered Hands Help Curb a Problem in Westwood." They quoted the Mayor, Norm Gaar as saying, "To many of these kids, $10 just means how long it takes them to talk the old man out of it. They don't remember the money. But they do remember mud out of the sewers, moving gravel with a shovel and cutting six foot weeds with a scythe."

I served as municipal judge for two years and when Norm decided to run for the Kansas Senate in 1965, I ran for Mayor and won, and I held that post for 21 great years. Norm won his Senate race too. And his help to Westwood as a Senator over the years was absolutely crucial to the city's success. He has been one of Westwood's best friends.

It was toward the end of the 1960s that our financial fortunes began to improve with the little bit of money we made came from property taxes and from what the court generated. One of our businesses at that time was Hallmark Cards which had a little building on what is now Shawnee Mission Parkway. They decided to move to Lawrence and that left us a vacant building.

I started working with realtors trying to get that space filled and I got a call one day from a realtor representing a company called United Utilities. I ended up meeting their president, Paul Henson, and eventually he agreed to move in with his 40 employees in April 1966. It was a nice utility company involved in telephone, natural gas and water, and first thing you know they started growing by leaps and bounds.

At that time there was a state statute on the books that required certain businesses to pay an intangible tax which is a property tax based on corporate stock dividends and interest. When that happened our city revenue went from the tens of thousands to the hundreds of thousands. The *Kansas City Star*, in an article on our eliminating city property taxes after United Utilities moved in, reported that our budget went from $63,000 in 1966 to $453,000 in 1970. All of a sudden we had more money than Carter had pills.

We started building sidewalks and improving streets and we bought the best police and maintenance equipment in the county. Sometime during that period United Utilities got rid of their water and gas interests and began to focus on communications. They changed their name to United Telecom, and as their fortunes continued to improve, so did Westwoods.

Today, of course, that company is known as Sprint, the huge international corporation which has chosen Johnson County as its global headquarters. A lot of people probably don't remember that there was a time when Sprint almost slipped through our fingers.

In the mid-1970s when I was chairman of the Johnson County Airport Commission, I heard through the grapevine that United Telecom was thinking of moving out. I called Paul Henson and asked him if that were true and he said yes that he was thinking of moving to the Country Club Plaza because they didn't have an intangible tax in Missouri.

I asked Paul if we got rid of the tax would he stay. He said Yes, and the first person I called was Norm Gaar, who was still in the Senate. With Norm's help and with the help of Senate President Dick Rogers, Gov. Bob Bennett, and Representatives Earl Ward from Mission Hills and Rex Hoy from Mission, we got the law changed so counties and cities didn't have to levy the entire tax if they didn't want to. We significantly lowered our rate and that's what kept Sprint in Kansas.

A lot of other good things started happening to Westwood about the time United Utilities moved here. The late 1960s and early 1970s those were really the years that Westwood grew up.

For example, it was in the late 1960s that Westwood acquired a piece of ground between 47th and 48th Streets and between State Line and Rainbow, where Woodside Racquet Club is now. It wasn't part of any city at the time. We referred to it as Dogpatch.

$37,000 Federal Revenue Sharing Check

The County Commission asked Westwood Hills if they had any interest in taking the land, but they didn't want it and eventually the county gave it to us. It had been owned by the Gas Service company, which had planned to build a corporate office building there. R. Crosby Kemper, Sr., told Gas Service if they moved out of Missouri to Westwood they'd have problems. So Gas Service sold it to a man named Clarence Goppert who was in the banking business.

We agreed to pay about $400,000 for the property. We leased the land to a developer who wanted to put up the Racquet Club and an office building. However the city subordinated the land for the project. The project was completed but the developer was unable to meet his principal and interest payments and GE Credit Corporation foreclosed on the property and the city's land. At that time the city formed the Westwood Foundation in order to issue industrial revenue bonds so we could purchase the development from GE.

We issued the bonds, finished the office development, and sold it to a private company. That left us with the Club which the city still owns today and which still generates a great deal of income.

Other accomplishments during the early 1970s included construction of a new school at 50th and Rainbow. The Westwood View School, where most of our kids had gone, had been built during the war and it was deteriorating. Finally the building was condemned. We got a school bond issue going, tore down the old school, and built the new one. It's still a very nice school now and part of the Shawnee Mission School District.

When we tore the old school down we salvaged an ornamental "WV" for Westwood View that had been cast out of masonry and placed on the brick facade of the school. That emblem was incorporated into a rock wall at the city park at 50th and Rainbow, where it remains today.

That park, built in the early 1970's was another major accomplishment during those glory years. It's still used every day, even in winter. It was also during the early 1970s that we bought land at 47th and Mission road that had been storage area for the Logan Moore Lumber Company. I think we paid about 50 cents a square foot. Eventually, Associated Wholesale Grocers bought the land from us and put up a grocery store. They also constructed their coupon redemption center with industrial revenue bonds. Velvet Cream popcorn also took advantage of IRBs to build their new facility on Belinder. If I remember correctly, we sold the Logan Moore property for $2.70 a square foot, so the city came out pretty well on that deal too.

Westwood enjoyed its 15 minutes of national fame in 1972, when Richard Nixon was still in office. The federal government had become involved in what was called federal revenue sharing to cities, which they don't do any more. One day, we got, unsolicited, an $37,000 check in the mail from the government. We were doing fine at the time and we didn't need the money, so we bundled it up and sent it back to them.

But the Feds wouldn't take it. They returned it to us. The morning after that happened I got a call from NBC out of Chicago. They wanted to interview me, and by the time 5 p.m. rolled around, I'd been contacted by all three networks and by newspapers from all over the country. I couldn't believe it. We were even mentioned on the Johnny Carson Show and in the *Readers' Digest*.

We eventually decided to distribute the money to all the cities in the county, based on population, but the Feds wouldn't let us do that. Well, at about that time Johnson County was starting up its Med-Act Service. We ended up using the money to buy Med Act's first ambulance, and we turned the title over to them. Ironically the first person hauled in it was Katherine Belinder, whose husband was from a very old Johnson County family. Belinder Road, which runs the entire length of Westwood, was named after them.

Westwood would never have flourished as it had without the involvement of a lot of great people who worked as a cohesive unit toward a single goal: Building a great community. I would encourage the citizens of Westwood to continue to take an active interest in their city, if not as an elected person then as a volunteer. I guarantee you'll never be sorry.

Even though I was Mayor of Westwood it's impossible for one person to handle on his own a city operation. I would like to take this opportunity to thank all of the council people and city employees who were as instrumental in seeing Westwood develop as I was. I'd like to make noted recognition of Norm Gaar, Ray Johnson, Gene Culbertson, George Keller, George Kiloh, George Brown and many others who have helped our community flourish.

William L. Kostar

In the April elections of 1986, our community was in a bit of turmoil. Some newer residents felt that decisions were being made in secret and that they had little input, and the election produced a split council of three old-guard, two new members. The meetings were sufficiently contentious that one of the old members resigned, and I was asked by Mayor Dennis to fill the unexpired term. Within the next two months I was elected Council President and then became Mayor upon Jamie Foster's resignation. It was interesting learning curve!

The Council worked well together and we made a focused effort on open meetings and communications with residents, commitments that remain important today. There were issues like Woodside being for sale, the pool sliding down the hill into Kansas city, and some staff turnover, but a team approach helped us prevail.

Within a couple of years we were able to pay the bonds on Woodside two years early and began to assess whether it made sense to get out of leased space and build our own city hall. The rent in 1989 was $90,000 annually, and the space was particularly inappropriate for the police department

William L. Kostar

Our approach involved a citizen's advisory committee to research the concept and select an architect, the Foundation, who devised the funding, and the City Council, who were the real owners. We still had to negotiate to buy additional property and later worked through some environmental cleanup on the site, but moved into the building in November 1990 and dedicated it on May 18, 1991. It's become a real focus, not just for Westwood. But for many other metro-wide organizations and events. I take my hat off to all the courageous people involved; it's quite an eye-opener to be signing documents committing to such an endeavor!

In 1989 the City also celebrated its Fortieth anniversary with a pancake breakfast by the Council, a parade, arts show, and other activities. Murray Maxwell, Westwood's former Mayor, was the Grand Marshall. The festivities were our biggest city-wide event to the point, and the efforts of the many volunteers produced a great time.

Our next major change was to consider becoming less dependent on Sprint for revenue. The company had been very good to Westwood, and relations remained cordial, but what had been a regulated utility was now in the very volatile long-distance business. Additionally, the city property and sales tax bases had grown, we owned our own building, and devised a financial plan to bridge us through payment of the city hall bonds. Sometimes you can make lemonade out of lemons, as we found out when interest rates fell and we went to the Kansas Legislature to get a law passed enabling the Foundation to invest in a conservative portfolio of stocks and bonds. Since then we have averaged more than 10% return per year, and a fund which was designed to decrease as it was used for city operations has actually grown while contributing about $100,000 in tax-cutting revenues. Again, it was a bold and complex move for such a small city, and many contributed their expertise and time. The rewards will be very long lasting.

Westwood has a reputation as a place run in a very business-like way, both by staff and elected officials. Additionally, we've played key roles in City, County and Metro-wide cooperative efforts, which have benefited our residents tremendously. I've been most gratified both personally and professionally, with all the great people I've had a chance to work with.

We have so many great volunteers in Westwood, we couldn't possibly do all the things we do without them. Easter egg hunts, city-wide garage sales, Oktoberfest, and all the boards and commissions activities make our town a satisfying and enjoyable place to live. We never lack for volunteers!

Finally, I look at the results of what we together have worked all the years to build. Government can play only a limited role with geography, economics, and even luck being a big part of what happens to a community. But we have to be pleased that Westwood businesses are expanding and new ones are moving in, our streets, sidewalks, and parks are well maintained, young families are moving into and raising kids in our community (Westwood View's kindergarten class in 1999 will be over

50), and our property values remain strong.

I'm very appreciative to have been given opportunities to serve the neighborhood where I've lived for over twenty years. It's been challenging fun, scary, time consuming, frustrating, and, finally enormously worthwhile.

William Kostar

Residents Remember Westwood

Marcus Pasley

Moving to Westwood In 1947

The City of Westwood, in the northeast part of Johnson County, Kansas, is a great place to live. I know, because I have lived in Westwood for over 51 years. Moved to this great little city two years before it was incorporated.

Returned from World war II in late 1946, anxious to get on with the life and wife waiting for me. One of our priorities was a house instead of an apartment and in early 1947 on a Sunday drive we decided Westwood was the neighborhood for us. The search was on and a chance turn on a narrow blacktop road led us north on Belinder and noticed a house being built stopped to take a look and when it was finished, in March, we moved in.

The narrow blacktop with dirt ditches and no sidewalks looked good to us and we loved our home. The area on the west side of Belinder and starting about 48th Street was almost bare. Very few houses. On the north side of our house is the Belinder house. This was the home place of an 800 acre farm at one time. In the back yard of the Belinder house there was a hand dug well. (Water was very good.) Just west of the well was a large barn, about the same location as 2707 west 47th, terrace (Mike Starrs'). Just south of the barn was a pond, the banks of which joined the northwest corner of 4752 Belinder (my home). On a line starting at the Belinder farm house and running due west to Mission road, then north to the county Line. Then east to Belinder Road, was a 6 acre size area that contained nothing but trees. Westwood's first mayor lived in the only house on that six acres, and was about 200 feet north of the Belinder house and was on Belinder also. Mr. Maxwell was a good mayor and was well thought of.

When we moved into our home the area was just starting to develop. Our home was the third in the development. Second was the house south of us and first was the house west of it. The developer then cleared the 6 acres mentioned above and built 19 homes in that area.

When the 6 acres was still a wooded area there was a branch starting at about 47th and Mission road (IGA Store). It ran south, slanting toward Belinder and came through just west of my back yard then turn southwest and emptying into a storm sewer at Belinder and 48th street. The developer filled the branch with fill dirt beginning at the north end of neighbors backyard. They then built house #1, my neighbors home, then #2, the house at Belinder and 48th and then #3 on Belinder. Our home.

The three new homes were soon filled with families and all was fine until it rained. Then the branch came back to life. It dumped water in my neighbors backyard (1) and his backyard joined my backyard (3). The water would get about 2 feet deep in his backyard before it was high enough to run over the lawns to the street and down the storm sewer. You could take a good boat ride in this area. One time the water broke the basement window of house #2 (2700 W. 48th.) and filled the basement up to the house floor. I helped the owner pump the water out, and considered what could be done, then built a stone wall on the south and west sides of my property.

The city did not have the money to build the needed storm sewer. So a bunch of us donated money to pay for a 30 inch sewer starting on 47th. Street Terrace west of Belinder and the same direction the branch ran and connected to the storm sewer on the north side of 48th street.

In the mid fifties we decided it would be handy to have a water well in the back yard for lawn use for the neighbors and us. The first 18 feet was regular drilling then we hit a limestone rock that was 33 feet thick, reassuring us that in this area Westwood is on a very, very solid foundation. At 225 feet we hit an ocean of water, and like the ocean it was very salty, We then decided to continue and maybe get a gas well. At 500 feet we hit the Bartlesville Oil sand and a gusher started to rumble up to the surface. The well was quickly shut to avoid spray from damaging the surrounding area. A party from Phillips Petroleum Co. looked it over and said it would make a very good well and a high producer. In making a search about the regulations for oil wells I discovered that any proceeds from the well for a certain distance had to be given to the owner of that property. In our case it checked out to be 27 houses. We decided to tap into the gas instead. Because it was within 15 BTU's of the city gas, we had to make no adjustments of any kind to use it. Also, piped gas to the Belinder house and to the Mike Starr home. We had free gas for a long time, till it was time to install a new pipe in the well. Due a mistake made in the installation, we closed the well, as the cost for correcting the mistake would pay city gas bills for a long time.

There are many stories about Westwood advancing the last fifty years. The has really moved forward. We have had good leadership. It is getting to be a better place to live each year. If you live in Westwood you are a very lucky person.

POLICE CHIEF ALLAN A. WRINKLE

AA Wrinkle was employed as an officer for the Police Department May 15, 1955. He served as officer until he was promoted to Police Sgt. July 1959. In August 1959 became the Police Chief. His retirement was May 1975. He had served the City of Westwood for a period of 20 years.

In June 1974, an in-car computer terminal was installed in the City's two patrol cars. Westwood was the first Johnson County city to provide this direct central computer in Kansas City Missouri Terminal in the city hall office that linked into the network. The bank of information had been available but the officer out in the car had to call a dispatcher's on his radio to ask for information and wait for the dispatcher vocal response.

In the new system the officer "types" his request on a keyboard mounted under the dashboard directly into the computer and his answer returns visually on a screen. The entire procession, from sending requests to receiving information, takes only about 7 seconds. At this time the system is used only for traffic regulations.

Projects promoted by Chief Wrinkle include the Life Line Children's Home. Dr. Harry E. Livermore served as Director. Marvin Gearheart was Home Life Director and Ethel Hardie, treasurer.

Chief Wrinkle had obtained permission to have a Christmas Party for the children at the home. Mrs. Eileen Wrinkle and Jim Melton joined in the idea. Arrangements were made to get a list of presents the children wanted for Christmas and some special articles needed for the home. Funds were donated by citizens and Businesses for the presents. Many volunteers made this project a success. The party was held at the Westwood View School with programs furnished by Special Musical Groups, choirs and Specialized stunts. Refreshments were then served and the best followed when Santa Claus

Police Chief Al Wrinkle proudly displays a new police cruiser fully eequipped with an early 1970's state-of-the-art computer terminal which the department had just purchased.

John Stover began to give out the presents. Gifts also given to the home were items such as sheets, pillowcases slips, towels, wash cloths, underwear, socks ,combs, deodorants, dishes, school supplies, canned juices, etc. This was done for several years until Life Line Children's Home moved

Chief Wrinkle also started a program for the younger boys of the community. They were named were named Westwood Rangers. The program was designed to teach the care and handling of weapons and to promote Good Relations between the boys and the Police Department and its officers. Safety , traffic signals especially bicycle riding, etc.

45

Westwood Rangers saw movies, had guest speakers from the FBI and other law enforcement agencies, and went on tours, including Saturday junkets to the Hudson ranch near Pomona, Kansas where the boys could spend the day hiking, eating and riding Shetland ponies. After three years the Rangers Club disbanded for the lack of adult assistance. Al next sponsored an Explorer Scout post for two years but again did not find sufficient adult help.

Chief Wrinkle's Westwood Rangers

CITY OF WESTWOOD
DEPARTMENT OF POLICE
THE BEARER Allan A. Wrinkle , IS HEREBY
RECOGNIZED AND IDENTIFIED AS President
WITH THE
CITY OF WESTWOOD. STATE OF KANSAS. ss

RANGERS

AL WRINKLE

HAS TAKEN THE PLEDGE SHOWN ON THE REVERSE SIDE AND
HAS SWORN TO UPHOLD IT.
DATE April 28, 1961
CHIEF OF POLICE   CHAIRMAN

Rangers Pledge Card (front and back)

RANGER'S PLEDGE

I, _____
PLEDGE TO BE FAITHFUL TO GOD. TO RESPECT AND DEFEND THE CONSTI-TUTION OF THE UNITED STATES. THE CONSTITUTION OF THE STATE OF KANSAS. AND THE ORDINANCES OF ALL CITIES:

TO RESPECT AND OBEY MY PARENTS:

TO ATTEND SCHOOL REGULARLY, AND ALWAYS STRIVE TO OBTAIN AN EDUCATION:

TO GIVE MY BEST IN ATHLETICS. AND ALWAYS PLACE FAIR PLAY AND HONOR ABOVE VICTORY:

TO TRY BY MY EXAMPLE OF RIGHT LIVING TO LEAD OTHERS TO DO RIGHT:

TO ASSIST THOSE IN TROUBLE:

TO RESPECT ALL LAW ENFORCEMENT OFFICERS, AND TO LOOK UPON THEM AS FELLOW OFFICERS AND FRIENDS:

TO RESPECT THE RIGHTS AND PROP-ERTY OF ALL PEOPLE.

During this time those that were involved saw a need for a better Boys Club in the county. They contacted the regional Chicago office of Boys' Clubs of America which agreed to send its regional director down to meet our community leaders.

Chief Wrinkle was made President of the Boys Club. This had been his dream for years. He began his missionary work presenting this to anyone that would listen. The question became where would they find a building large enough to handle what one should have to make it worthwhile. Mr. Harry Betz became most interested, and a retired air conditioning man, who had his own plane, took other interested men and flew to others boys clubs to see how they were operated. Things began to fall in place.

Mr. Roy Kahn, owner of Guaranteed Foods, Inc. owned the Food Locker Building at 5240 Belinder Avenue in Fairway. He was using the building for storage and an electrical appliances salesroom in the front interior. Chief Wrinkle told the Board of Directors about the building and stated Mr. Kahn had offered the two-store building for $1.00. This became the first site of the Boys' Club in Johnson County

Construction was started immediately for several rooms for each age to have things they would be interested in such as ping-pong, pool, shuffleboard, cards, checkers, crafts, woodwork workshops, printing shop, snack bar, kitchens, showers, dressing room, a gymnasium which includes basket ball, weight lifting, boxing, judo and physical fitness, a ham radio shop, photo lab chapel and lounge. They would have a chance to do their homework with friends and under the supervision of teachers who had already volunteered. It would give the boys a place to go through informal guidance, and improve them physically, mentally and in character.

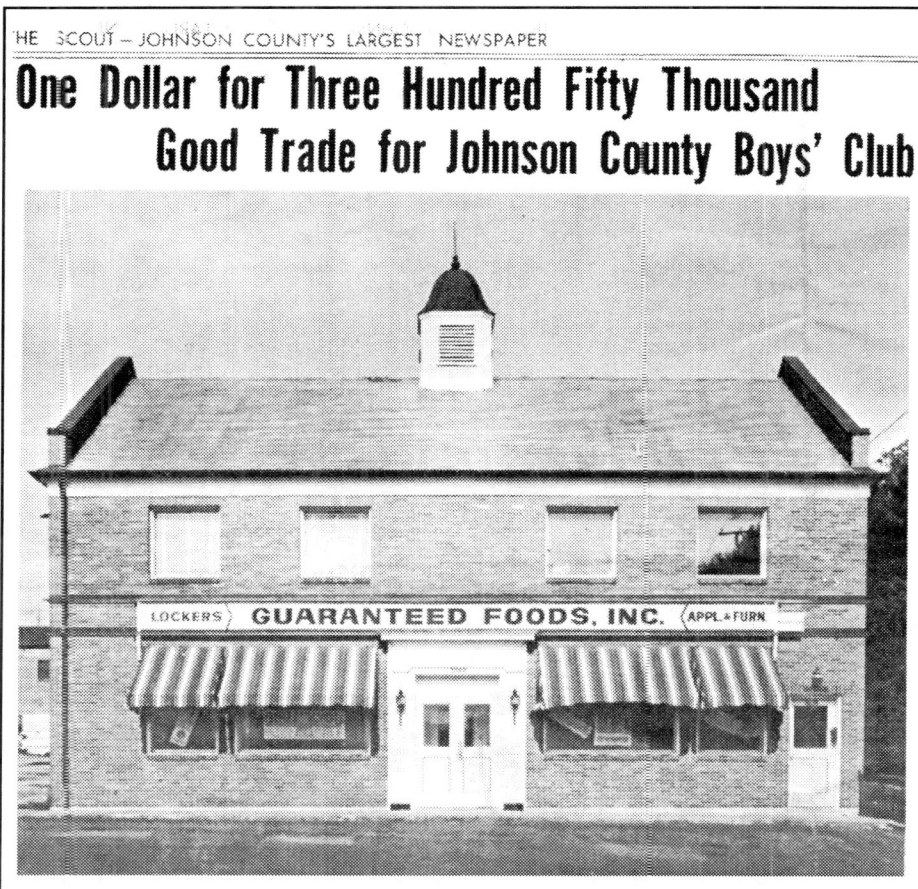

THE SCOUT – JOHNSON COUNTY'S LARGEST NEWSPAPER

One Dollar for Three Hundred Fifty Thousand Good Trade for Johnson County Boys' Club

Benefits from the Fund Drive for the Club included the movie "Gone With the Wind" at the Glenwood Theater. This was the first showing of to be seen in color and on a wide screen with full stereophonic sound. Mrs. Wrinkle was chairman of the ticket sales and office secretary of the Club.

The biggest fund drive to raise money was performed by the Old Mission Jaycees, who made a deal with Sid Morris of the Allen's Drive-in located at 2522 Johnson Drive. The entire gross proceeds from the sale of food and beverages at the drive-in would be donated to the Club building operating funds, time would be on Saturday from 11:00 am until 2:00 am.

Many Rummage Sales were held. Many people and businesses donated money, even pool tables. Ned Gallagher, owner of Hobby Haven in Mission, donated a 90-foot slot race track course and Joseph R. Hurd, Mission Police Chief, donated three cars for the race track. The Shawnee Mission Pilot Club, in a ceremony at the South Overland Park Shopping Center, donated money received from a fountain in which coins had been thrown from a balcony.

The Directors' wives, better known as the Auxiliary, were working to raise money for the Club.

The Boys Club was begun in 1966. An alarming rise in juvenile delinquency prompted plans for a Johnson County Boys Club.

A growing number of teenagers had violated laws because of an abundance of idle time and spending money. Exclusively for boys ages 8 through 18 it was nonsectarian in organization management, leadership to its members. The club was open every weekday afternoon and evenings and on weekends. Five police chiefs of suburban and ex urban Johnson County areas were members of the Boys Club of Johnson County Board of Directors. Dues were $1.00.

A BIG STEP TOWARD THE FIRST BOYS' CLUB OF JOHNSON COUNTY was made when a dollar bill was exchanged for the deed to a building at 5240 Belinder. William E. Avery (left), treasurer of the Boys' Club board, is shown as he holds the deed after presenting the dollar bill to Roy L. Kahn (third from right), president of Guaranteed Foods, Inc., owners of the building. Others watching the transaction are, from left: Mayor Joe D. Dennis of Westwood; Harry D. Betz, chairman of major gifts committee; Mrs. Mary Old, news editor the Herald, who has taken an active interest in the Boys' Club project; Mayor Neale R. Peterson of Fairway, and Allan A. Wrinkle, Westwood Chief of Police, president of board.

EAT HAMBURGERS TO HELP BOYS — Among the dignitaries who attended the one-day food and fun fest at a Westwood drive-in were Larry Winn, left, Republican candidate for congress from District 3, and State Senator Norman Gaar of Westwood. All proceeds were given to the Building Fund of the first Boys' Club of Johnson County.

Ed Charles, third baseman for the Kansas City A's, and Jim Tyrer of the Chiefs were on hand to talk to the hundreds of youngsters who crowded around them. Joe Dennis, Mayor of Westwood and a member of Old Mission Jaycees, sponsor of the event, also greeted the patrons.

The project added $1,155.18 toward the $350,000 goal for the Boys' Club Building fund and operational expenses for the next three years. The club at 5240 Belinder is expected to open in early 1967.

Mrs. Eileen Wrinkle was not only was busy with the projects of her husband, but managed to do volunteer work though out the City of Westwood, such as the Meals on Wheels Program and as chairman of the Fund Raising for the Cancer and Heart Association. She became their Field Representative for Eastern and Southeastern Kansas.

New Executive Director Named for Cancer Unit

Mrs. Eileen Wrinkle, 2805 West Forty-eighth street, Westwood, has been named the new executive director of the Johnson County unit of the American Cancer society. The office is at 5880 Horton street, Mission.

Mrs. Wrinkle has served 15 years as a volunteer and has been a member of the board of directors seven years. She was serving as board chairman.

She was the Johnson County crusade chairman in 1970 and had been reappointed for the 1971 drive. In order to accept the new paid position, Mrs. Wrinkle resigned as board chairman and crusade chairman.

MRS. EILEEN WRINKLE

She worked as a volunteer for the American Cancer Society in the Johnson County area for 15 years. She served as house-to-house worker and worked up to Chairman of the Board of Directors a volunteer for 17 years before accepting the position as Executive Director of the Johnson County Unit of that organization in 1970 and served in the capacity until her resignation in 1973.

She worked for 13 years with the Life Line Children's Home and helped her husband with planning and putting on an Annual Christmas Party. In between other employment she was self-employed as a dressmaker. She also worked in the organization of the Boys Club of America. There, she was in charge of the bookkeeping, the fund raising and any work of the general office.

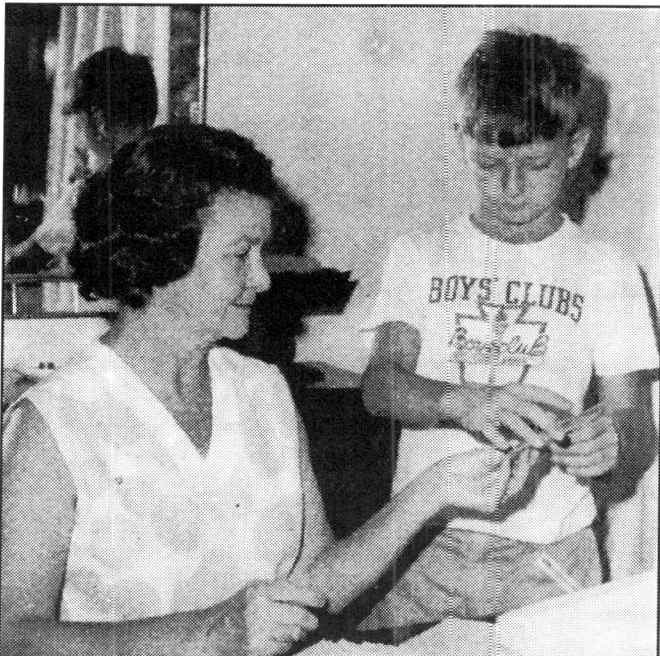

Mrs. Al Wrinkle, 2805 W. 48th St., and son Allan are pictured mailing tickets for the County premiere showing of "Gone With the Wind" Nov. 7, 1967 at Glenwood Theatre. Allan, 10, is a fifth grader at Westwood View school and is one of a group of boys who have contributed many hours of work on the boy's club along with adult volunteers. Sponsors of the Boy's club hope many area adults will call for tickets to the movie premiere.

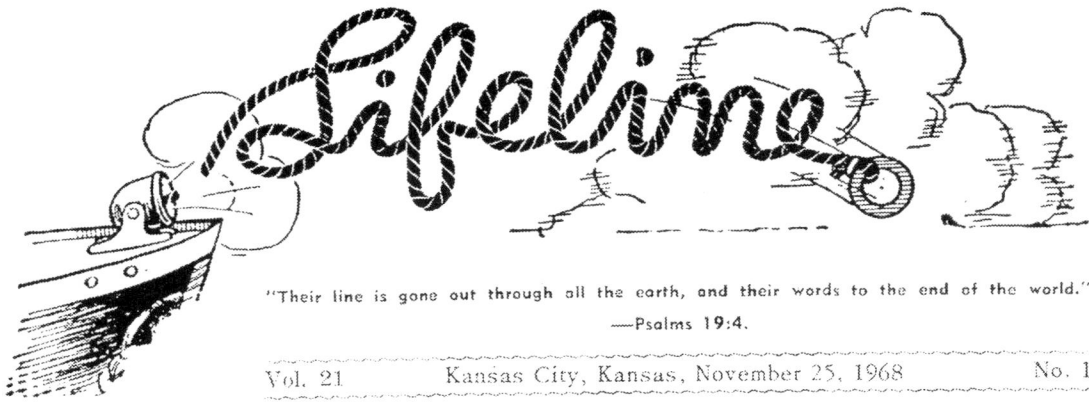

"Their line is gone out through all the earth, and their words to the end of the world."
—Psalms 19:4.

Vol. 21   Kansas City, Kansas, November 25, 1968   No. 12

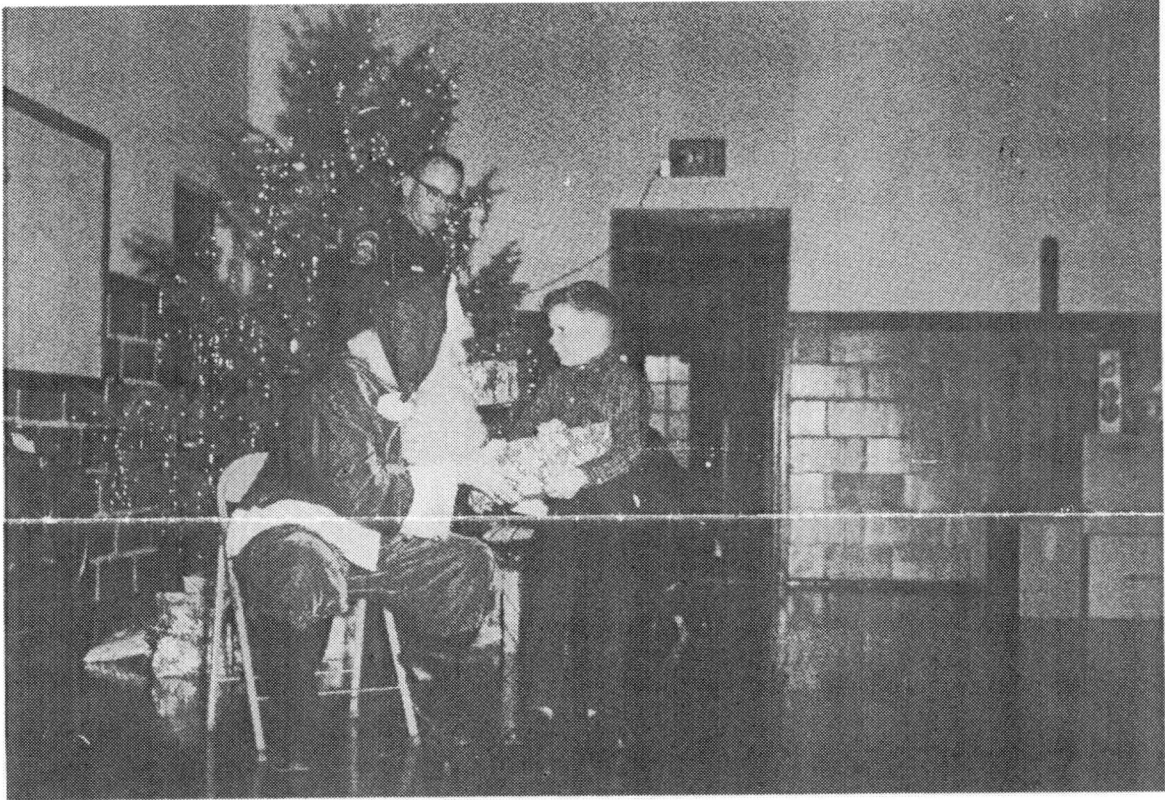

From: Ray Johnson

In 1958, my wife Charlotte and I, and two children, Jennifer and Christopher, moved to Westwood, Kansas.

Ray Johnson

In 1965 I was appointed to the Planning Commission by the Mayor of Westwood. In 1967 I was elected to the City Council and held that position for 16 years.

During these years I served as chairman of the Public Works Committee. When I ran for election one of my promises were to rebuild Mission Road. At that time it was a narrow two-lane, boardered by deep ditches. It was dangerous to the children walking to school. We worked hard to achieve this project and you can see the results. During the term in Public Works, we worked with Kansas City, Kansas, to widen and pave 47th Street from Mission Road to Rainbow Blvd. Rainbow Blvd. was totally resurfaced, Belinder Road was totally redone and new storm sewers were included. Numerous other streets and sidewalks were completed. We built the beautiful Park at 50th Street and Rainbow Blvd. We inaugurated the fall leaf pick up which was a great benefit to our citizens. It was great fun to see the many changes in the way our city looked.

The Mayor appointed me chairman of the Police Committee and we then brought it up to the 20th Century. I am very proud we were able to turn our City into a first-rate place to live and on which property values have been maintained.

From: Willard E. Oldberg

I served on the City Council of Westwood for nine years and I remember many things that the residents of Westwood had and still have.

I remember that Westwood was referred to as one of the richest cities due to the income from United Telecom Co. This company was persuaded to come to Westwood by Joe Dennis, the Mayor, Ray Johnson and Senator Norman Gaar.

The income from the intangible tax provided funds to buy good equipment for the Public Works Department, and repair and maintain the streets and curbs throughout the City. The stone walls, where needed, were elegantly done, and add much to the beauty of the City.

I served on the City Council when we voted to build the Woodside Racquet Club and the building on 47th Street and State Line. I remember how so many people were opposed to this, but we proceeded even when we knew it would jeopardize our political careers.

We had good people on the council - Nancy Jeffries, George Kiloh and I all wanted to do the right thing for Westwood.

As you all know, the corner of 47th and Rainbow, where the City Hall is today, was purchased for commercial purposes. It is the ideal location for the City Hall and the City is an independent entity today.

I remember Nancy Jefferies planting trees in the City, and it is wonderful to see the tree lined streets today.

I remember the city park: We were criticized for installing a fountain, which was feared inoperable in time, but 25 years later it is still working. The corner of 47th and Mission Road, which also has a fountain, has enhanced the corner by the IGA Grocery Store. It is an attractive asset for that area and was done without the cooperation of other cities who benefit from the enhancement.

One of the best people Westwood had back then was Gene Culbertson, the City Clerk. Her expertise kept Joe Dennis, Ray Johnson and me in line, which she did very well. If all facts were known, she really ran the City in the way it was supposed to be run.

I wish the City of Westwood lots of luck in the future and hope it can continue to be one of the best run cities in the nation.

Willard Oldberg

From: George Keller

My family has been in the seed, hardware and nursery business for two generations. It followed I would also like to be in the nursery business. So I rented the building and lot at the corner of 47th Ter. and Rainbow from Wayne and Elizabeth Wrightsman in November of 1944, and sold Christmas trees. As spring came around I started a garden center. The office had been a barber shop. I added a back and then a bath house. The building didn't have any plumbing. There was a outhouse set on a little hill behind the office. We had a bulldozer come in and level the vacant lot so we could utilize the ground. We tied onto the water line of the house to the south side of the office. Later on we got sewers and a direct water line.

We purchased a vacant lot across from the nursery from John and Grace Glayer and built a utility building on the west end of the lot. Later on we leased the ground but kept the building. A company built a nice building with good parking on the rest of the lot. In the meantime we purchased the property south of the nursery and our family, except for our son George, was born and raised there. Later on we purchased the Nickols property that was east of our house and the Triplett house east of the Nickols house. After Elizabeth Wrightsman passed away the Wrightsmans offered to let us purchase the nursery lot, the brick house and the Wrightsman home. Sometime later June Wrightsman told us she had a buyer for all our property. We made a deal and Rainbow Nursery was history.

Our children were born and raised in our old house and we have so many fond memories.

We donated a Christmas tree to every home in Westwood View School as long as we were in business.

We also donated a Christmas tree to all the police officers every year.

I was also Westwood's Civil Defense Director for several years. I was so relieved when they built the new school with a tornado shelter capacity.

I served as councilman for Westwood from 1957 to 1971, when I was defeated. I still have most of the certificates of election.

OLDEST BUSINESS PREDATES CITY

Westwood is now 25 years old. But the business that has remained under the same ownership within the city limits for the longest period of time is even older.

Rainbow Nursery, 4740 Rainbow, was opened by George Keller in December, 1944, and he and his family have operated it ever since.

Through the years, Keller said, "Things haven't really changed. We've always sold shrubs, trees, plants, and the things to care for your garden. And it's always been a tremendous area for our products."

He recalls that there was then a grocery store just across the street and a few other businesses around, but no homes beyond the Skelly service station.

Keller explained that his location on Rainbow gives him "a unique spot. There is really no competition to the north of us for quite a ways and there's a great interest in gardening and care of lawns and trees here. Westwood has a lot of beautiful trees. Most of the material we sell here is replacement materials and care products."

Even in this established area of longtime gardeners, Keller noted an increases interest in gardening this year. "More people are interested, it seems."

This interest grows despite what Keller says are greater price increased in the last two or three years than every before. "Nursery stock and plants don't go up in price so much. But the garden care products, the ones that use the same petroleum derivatives the farms use, those have really gone up."

Keller entered the nursery business quite naturally. "My father has the Keller Nursery in Kansas City, Kansas, which he started in 1925. Before that grandpa was in the seed business."

The younger Kellers? They just might carry on the family tradition. "I have a daughter who just graduated from Johnson County Community College with honors, and a son who graduated from Shawnee Mission North. I have one son in the nursery and one who is a landscaper."

The Kellers have lived next door to the nursery since 1953. They have expanded into a partnership in the Overland Park Nursery and the operation of a seasonal satellite business, Flower World, U.S.A., open only in the early spring.

During his life in Westwood, Keller has been active in the community. He served for 10 years on the city council. He is happy that this is the site he chose for his nursery and garden store.

"I'm delighted to be a part of this town".

George Keller

4740 Rainbow Blvd., Westwood KS ~ 1942

4740 Rainbow Blvd., Westwood KS 66205

From: Bill Latz

As the City of Westwood approaches it's fiftieth birthday, I can reminisce thirty years ago when we moved to Westwood with our five children - how fortunate to be within walking distance of the grade school and high school of our choice. Our children have since left the nest, but Peggy and I have no intention of leaving - too many great memories and great neighbors!

Although, I was a council member for a few years my most memorable experience was being a member of the original Westwood Foundation whose initial responsibility was to salvage the facilities of the Racquet Club - and office building to the east whose developers were facing imminent foreclosure. The city had subordinated the land to the loan so we had a vested interest. We met weekly for the next few years seeking tenants and directing interior construction for the sparsely occupied office building.

Under the astute leadership of long-time mayor, Joe Dennis our mission was accomplished just short of the deadline - the office building was sold and the Racquet Club refinanced. I'll always remember Joe's favorite motto: "I'd rather ask for forgiveness than permission." It fit him so well!

Fortunately the city has continued to be blessed with outstanding progressional leaders like Bill Kostar, council members, and chief "Corky" Wells. Thanks for making this a "great place to live!"
Bill Latz
2703 West 50th Terr
Shawnee Mission, Kansas 66205

Woodside Racquet Club

From: Rosemarie Bader

We moved here in 1963 to be near St. Agnes Church and School. I remember the shops along Belinder and 50 Highway before United Telecom (now Sprint), the hardware store, cleaners and the furniture store and don't forget

The "original" Fine Arts Theatre at 2820 West 53rd Street gave residents a place to see first run movies. In later years, Wolferman's, Houston's and now Fairway Grill all used the location as eating establishments. What we know as the Fine Arts Theatre in Mission today has no connection with the Fairway establishment. It was orininally the Dickinson Theatre.

Ragans Dari Q and King's Food Host. On the east side of King's was a liquor store and beauty shop. It was really a handy shopping area.

Does anyone remember Harry Worde, a good neighbor. He was always looking out his front window checking to see if any strange cars were in the area.

The little rock house across from St. Agnes Church was at one time Horner's Riding Academy.

Looking forward to reading more about Westwood that I cannot remember.

Rosemarie Bader

From: Robert E. Flaspohler

The voters of the City of Westwood elected me to a term on the City Council, and I appreciate their confidence in me. I hope that I served faithfully and earned that confidence. It was a rewarding experience that this "Rookie Politician" enjoyed. The time I served under the excellent leadership of Mayor Joe Dennis and the expertise of City Clerk Gene Culbertson left many pleasant memories. Again, thanks for the memories -

Robert E. Flaspohler

From: Jackie Bays

I grew up on the Missouri side of State Line. In 1955 I found Westwood to be the closet small community to the "big city." Over the many years, there have been many changes in Westwood. My street was a dead end with a farm, including a friendly cow, at its end. The farm would eventually be replaced by 12 new houses and the street was cut through to Belinder. My oldest son went to the "old" Westwood View School and my other child attended the present school which we Westwood residents paid for. Then came unification. Westwood View has always seemed like "our" school. About 10 years ago a group got together and started a Body Recall exercise group which met at the Westwood Christian Church. When the new City Hall was built they offered an exercise time, but the church was carpeted? From a group of 12 we have dwindled to a handful of regulars. But we are determined not to grow old but remain young with Westwood.

M. J. (Jackie) Bays

Westwood, a City of Qualities

From: Vicki M. Ross

Years ago Mike and I knew the old "Quality House" in Westwood with its giant cottonwood tree was the place for us. As I reminisce about the past 21 years, I think about the qualities of Westwood that encourage us to stay.

Quality #1: A Strong Sense of Community

Twenty years ago, the school board announced plans to close Westwood View School. Within days of the announcement, Westwood residents and business owners joined forces to stop the plan. Today, Westwood View is a thriving school because of a strong sense of community then and now.

It was also a strong sense of community that placed Westwood ahead of many cities as an accessible city. Many years before the Americans with Disabilities Act was legislated and with disabled persons living in the city, accessibility for all residents was a prominent concern with each street and municipal building renovation. It was no accident. A strong sense of community guaranteed the accessibility of the new city hall.

Quality # 2: Proactive

In this day and age of immediate gratification, planning for the future is rarely rewarded. As the city of Westwood grew, so did a little technology company known today a Sprint. Through the aid of an intangibles tax, Sprint "financed" a large part of the city budget. There were those who were concerned about a future financial uncertainty. Politicians living for today might have made the argument to leave the situation as is, but members of the city council, like their constituents, did not. They took action to secure the financial future of the city. It was an honor and a pleasure to serve as a city councilwoman during that process. Removing the intangibles tax and equalizing the tax base were decisions for the future.

Quality #3: Environmental Awareness

Rarely will one find a placard in Westwood proclaiming the benefits of environmental protection. However, the message is clear: environmental awareness has a fundamental role in policy making. Trees are plentiful in the city and to insure the future of a tree city, new saplings are planted each year.

Waste minimization is also a goal for the city. The Westwood Neighborhood Association was founded by a group of residents interested in maintaining and improving the quality of the city. Through the collaborative efforts of the Westwood Neighborhood Association and members of the city council, a curbside recycling and composting program was developed, the first in the state.

Quality # 4: Village Ideals

Stability is a value that many seek and never find. In Westwood, it is common occurrence. Living in the same house for 21 years would be marked as an unusual event in other cities. Twenty-one years of living in Westwood marks us as "newcomers" behind people who were here before the city was incorporated.

The stability of our neighborhood brings special benefits. Our children have many "parents and grandparents" who watch out for them and give them advice. As parents, we have been blessed by neighbors who share similar values. Our children not only hear about the importance of values, they see generosity, honesty, tolerance, and hard work enacted each day by our neighbors. Our children have seen the importance of sharing time and talents and they have special memories of elderly neighbors who shared a part of their life. In the words of some, "it takes a village to raise a child." Those words are a part of life in Westwood.

Westwood is a small city in an urban area. Residents know their neighbors and watch out for them. They are proactive. The people of Westwood push the politics of the here and now aside and make decisions that will insure the characteristics we seek in a city for the future.

As we prepare for the 50th birthday celebration of the city, I remember a similar celebration 10 years ago. It began with a suggestion by one person to recognize the history and accomplishments of 40 years. The celebration 10 years ago was a huge success because of the people who live and work in Westwood. With an additional 10 years of history and pride, the 50th celebration promises to be the biggest yet.

WHY, HOW AND WHEN I BECAME A WESTWOOD RESIDENT

From: Melvin Bond

I have been a Johnson County resident all of my 76 years. I started June 8, 1943 to work for LD Gates Co., a bus line contract carrier for *Kansas City Star* in eastern Kansas at 43rd and Rainbow. Single people like me lived in rented sleeping rooms close to work. I used to get my car serviced at Orville Bicking Service Station on the highway where, now Sprint Headquarters is located. I told Orville I would like to buy a lot for a future home. He told me of one next to him on the east owned by Mr. and Mrs. Selles, but didn't know if they were interested in selling it. I talked to them and they decided to sell to me in spring, 1949.

The Korean War came along and I already had plans for a house. I decided I would build while I could get material. My father, a carpenter, used my plan for my sister and husband in Raytown in spring of 1950 and as soon as we had their house done I started mine in October, 1950. I was still in a sleeping room at my aunt's and uncle's home. So after I finished it, I decided to buy a few pieces of furniture and moved in August 1, 1951.

In the late 50s some close friends retired to Commanche, Oklahoma and during visits with them while I was still single, they wanted me to meet this real nice girl, Mary Beth Dyer. Well it happened in September, 1959 and three months later we were married. This union produced two sons Gary, born January 1961, and Alan, born June 1963. Both boys - Gary's first year was in old Westwood View building, all 12 years in Shawnee Mission North District. Eagle Scouts Troop 192 graduates. Gary is now an Architectural Engineer and Alan is in Computer Science.

The first years of Mary's and my marriage were sort of lonesome for her as she had no relatives in Kansas. She got involved in genealogy and spent countless hours doing research, writing letters and visiting libraries. All our vacations included some research. Gary and Alan saw one court house and cemetery after another. This also got Mary into DAR - UDC Colonial Dames, all of which she was deeply involved with all her life.

As a stay at home mom, as other girls in Westwood were, she helped organize the Westwood Garden Club and was the first President in 1969. About this same time a man named Mr. Hoffman came to our door - his company in KCK was on strike at the time he was working out of Boy Scout office. Our Cub Pack 3193 was dead at the time. He and Mary, with help of other mothers at school, got the pack started up again and was quite successful. The last two years Alan was a cub we had a baseball team which was sort of wild but a lot of fun on the vacant lot were IGA is now. Do any of you remember mothers and fathers playing the boys that last day of the season?

Mary also served on the City Planning Commission. I feel the girl I brought from Oklahoma was quite an asset to our city and community, the girl that made my house a home and all my neighbors seem like family.

The piece of dirt I bought in 1949 where you could hear a cow moo and a rooster crow over the hill east of me has all changed but still is the best place I know to live. Thanks to all in Westwood.

Melvin Bond

AH, WESTWOOD! HOW WELL I REMEMBER!

From: Pebble Horn

In 1955, My husband George and I purchased a home on 51st Terrace a few doors from then Mayor Joe Dennis. In 1975, I closed my real estate brokerage office, retired and went home to putter around my house. As neighbors are inclined to do in Westwood, Mayor Dennis wandered over to chat one day, interrupting my yard work; he explained to me his plans to create the Westwood Foundation as an arm of the city, whose objective would be to solve Westwood's then problem of saving from financial foreclosure the Woodside Racquet Club and the adjacent four-story office building, the Westwood Plaza Towers. While the Racquet Club was doing well, its land was tied in control of the mortgage holder for the entire complex.

Plans were already under way to regain control of the project to benefit Westwood, and Mayor Dennis was confident the complex could be recaptured, though it might be a scramble, as indeed it was. Mayor Dennis asked me to help after the legal battle was over. He also tapped Bill Latz, another Westwood resident, to serve as Vice President of this new City-owned Foundation. Norman Gaar, Attorney and Westwood resident, added his skills to the legal tangle.

Since I didn't have much to do except dig out an occasional dandelion from my yard, I told the Mayor I would help. The meetings began. For dozens of hours I watched Mayor Dennis, Attorney Gaar, and others representing Westwood's interests, scrap with the mortgage holder and the then building owners.

Pebble Horn

Some days were tough. Mayor Dennis indicated Bill Latz and I could sit in this conflict since, after it was solved, we could then get to work to solve the huge vacancy situation in the Westwood Plaza Towers office building. Not only was there a substantial part of the building unoccupied, as is the case with new construction, but the available space was not "office-ready" - no ceiling, no lighting, no floor covering, no air/heat duct work, no partitions, etc. I spent everyday in the building trying to generate new tenants, expanding existing tenants, and determining their construction requirements. The office paper records, including construction records of the Racquet Club and office building, were dumped in piles on the floor of a vacant space. All this had to be pulled together.

The Foundation officers met regularly and often, making decisions that would shape the character of the building and at the same time recapture this project as a valuable asset for Westwood. Financially at times, it was a struggle, but 18 months after we won the right to try to pull the project from foreclosure, the Westwood Plaza Towers Office Building was fully completed and occupied by paying tenants. I then returned to my yard work.

For a while I missed meeting with Joe, Bill and Norma, but it was very satisfying to know the initial mission of the Westwood Foundation had been accomplished. Members of this Foundation were volunteers. As I hear of all the good things the Foundation is doing, I'm glad to have had a small part in its beginning.

Later, at the request of Mayor Bill Kostar, I served on the Board of Zoning Appeals, and as a member of a Committee to select and examine proposals to build a new City Hall. In connection with the latter assignment, I personally visited several area City Halls: Fairway, Mission, Prairie Village, Shawnee, and Grandview. I know other members of the committee made their own searches.

Westwood's corner at 47th and Rainbow was selected as the site for the new City Hall. That corner was then an unattractive, unproductive eyesore. The City Hall Committee examined in detail some 13 to 14 construction proposals before selecting one to build the attractive efficient City Hall/ Police Department you have today. Sure beats renting, doesn't it?

Unfortunately after 36 years in Westwood and suffering the great loss of my husband, I no longer wanted the responsibility of owning a home. I now live in a retirement complex in Overland Park.

I will always remember my Westwood days with fond memories.

CONGRATULATIONS Westwood!

Pebble Horn

A CURMUDGEON'S VIEW OF WESTWOOD

From: Jack W. Vetter

Like it or not, I am a lot older than I once was. This does give one a certain perspective in looking at the past. Westwood, Kansas, is a new city, even for the USA. However, certain memories generated in the short life of the area and in my life stand out. They stand out because of the contrast and difference between then and now.

My family moved to the Westwood area near the end of World War II, long before there was the City of Westwood. The most noteworthy features to my mind, in my small world, were the KMBC radio towers, Westwood View School and the small Fairway Shopping Center.

One feature in particular seems most telling of the change already underway: There was a small culvert crossing Belinder approximately at the west entrance to the current Sprint property, by the Fairway Shops. At that culvert was a sign stating "TRACTORS WITH LUGS PROHIBITED". This cryptic message referred to farm tractors with all-steel wheels. The drive wheels were supplied with cleats riveted to them for traction in muddy fields. There must have been a problem with the cleats tearing up pavement in those days.

The Fairway Shops faced the two-lane brick Highway 10 which wound through Mission, Merriam and Shawnee and out into the countryside. Crown Drug with its soda fountain occupied the corner spot by Belinder. On down the row were various businesses including the Dime Store, Zitron's grocery, the A&P, and finally the Fairway Theater. The Safeway had the Northeast corner at Belinder and the "Highway". "Blackie" had the D-X gas station at the Y-intersection. The only continuity that comes to mind is there is still a grocery in the A&P spot and Noble now operates a station where the old DX stood.

The Radio Towers still stand although sheep are no longer used to keep the grounds mowed. Brink's farm occupied the west side of Belinder, roughly between 50th and 51st Street. This was, I think, part of an old Indian land grant property, and was inhabited by Frank Brink and his mother. They kept cows, chickens and guinea pigs and certainly posed an interesting rustic contrast to the new suburban housing surrounding the property. There was also a Brink property just north of Sprint. I can recall seeing quail in those woods. "Old man" Brink was a familiar sight on the streets driving his old AA Ford stakebed truck with his Fox Terrier riding shotgun.

Sadly, the original Westwood View School is no more. Its proud masonry walls ornamented with terra cotta, its bow-string trusses, the whole works apparently fell victim to some phase of educational philosophy. It was replaced with an anonymous-looking building and a large parking lot. Of course, when I attended the school, automobiles were one to a family. The pupils walked not only to and from school, at the start and end of the school day, most walked home for lunch. I can only recall two students that were driven to and from school.

Perhaps my most indelible grade school memories are as follows:
1. The gathering of the whole school in the main entrance hallway around a huge Christmas tree to sing carols. How non-PC of us all. There was only one Jewish kid in school that I recall, and he apparently just accepted this celebration of Yuletide.
2. The smartest aleck in school being held upside-down by the ankles out a second story window and being shaken. This might create quite a stir if done today. But I felt he probably richly deserved it then, and still feel the same way now.
3. The entire school sitting down on the hardwood gym floor watching the blue glow of a floor model television operating on the stage of the gym. Television was very new and everyone was given the opportunity to watch the most important event in months: The World Series!

All these memories are from another world. They show how much change has taken place in our little precinct of the nation. Westwood was once on the edge of the built-up city. Then it became one starting point for the post-World War II suburban growth, or sprawl, to some. Now it must concern itself with maintaining its physical condition against deterioration.

In any case, the changes have come. What progress has occurred is harder for me to see.

GROWING UP IN WESTWOOD, KANSAS – 1936-1947

From: Midge Myers Miller

I moved to Westwood, Kansas, with my father and mother, Glenn and Eleanor Myers, in August of 1936 when I was not quite three years old. The unusually hot weather that summer had attracted my parents to the house on Mission Road between 51st Street and 51st Street Terrace. This particular two story house had a row of elm trees along the south side. There were practically no other trees in the whole neighborhood. My father put a rope swing in one of the elm trees which my friends and I enjoyed often. Across the street was a 27 hole golf course. The house on the corner of Mission Road and 51st Street belonged to Dr. and Mrs. Price. A vacant lot was on the other corner. During World War II this lot was used by several families in the neighborhood as a victory garden.

As a young child my neighborhood was basically my home and the homes on 51st Street from Mission Road east to the top of the hill. Dr. and Mrs. Price who lived next door were special friends of mine. I loved to visit them. To let Mrs. Price know that I was the one at the back door I was taught not to knock but rather to scratch on the screen with a spoon. If Mrs. Price did not have time to be with me, she simply could fail to answer the door and I would soon leave. Listening to Mrs. Price play the organ in her living room was a special treat for me. I knew no one else who owned an organ.

Up 51st Street lived three friends of mine, Sara Jane Snyder and Sandra and Sue Bosley. We spent much time playing in each others' yards or playing with dolls and paper dolls in our homes. Catching grasshoppers in the daylight or fireflies at night were frequent activities.

Sara Jane and I had a knack for finding adventure. When my father left out the paint he was using on our picket fence, we dipped our arms in it up to our elbows and said we were wearing long white gloves. My mother was not thrilled when faced with the clean up job. Sara Jane and I were also intrigues with the bull in the pasture behind her yard. Once in a while we would climb the fence and start walking towards the bull. As soon as it looked at us, we would head for the fence.

Besides having a bull near by another sign of the semi-rural nature of this area was our septic tanks in place of sewers. I have a vivid memory of septic tanks. The grease trap of our septic tank had to be dug up and cleaned when I was five or six years old. While the grease trap was uncovered, I was out in the back yard all dressed to go out with my parents and watching a bird. Suddenly the bird moved in the tree overhead so I stepped backwards and fell into the grease trap. We went no where that afternoon.

As I grew a little older, my neighborhood grew to include more children both girls and boys with whom I played hide and seek and kick the can. The Fourth of July was noisy with firecrackers from dawn until late at night. My friends and I shot off firecrackers in the day time and other fireworks at night. They were sold at many stores in the State of Kansas. The Fourth of July was the only time of year when we had soda pop at home. For this special day my mother always bought a small carton of Orange Crush. The other times I had soda pop were with friends at the drug store in Fairway where I usually ordered cherry Coke.

The Myers' home, at 5105 Mission Road, cost $6,500 when it was built in August 1936

Pets were an important part of my life in Westwood. For sixteen years I had a dog named Josephine. She would let me dress her in doll clothes and wheel her around in a doll buggy. She got along very well with Peep the duck I received one Easter and kept for two or three years. Peep lived in a dog house in our back yard and became quite a pet. When members of the family came into the back yard, she would run to us and stretch her neck out so we could pet her. Finally my parents decided we had kept Peep long enough and she was taken to join other ducks at Loose Park.

The two schools attended by girls and boys in Westwood were Westwood View Grade School and Shawnee Mission High School. At that time there was one high school in the area and no junior high or middle school. Westwood View was a two story brick building with one class for each grade kindergarten through eighth grade. One thing I remember about the school was the dioramas that lined the upstairs hall. These presented the history of people in the United States from the Indians onward. Recess was spent on swings, jumping rope, or playing basketball or baseball. When we got into the upper grades, a favorite activity for girls on the school ground was trading playing cards. Girls always wore dresses to school.

Social activities in the eighth grade included ballroom dancing lessons at a studio on the Plaza. Almost everyone in the class took the lessons. Then some of us had parties with dancing in our homes.

I remember three teachers from Westwood View who were there for many years. Mrs. Riggs taught kindergarten, Miss Fisher taught seventh grade and Miss Anderson taught eighth grade. A tradition at eighth grade graduation was having Miss Fisher sing "Bless This House." With graduation from eighth grade and entrance into Shawnee Mission High School in Merriam, Kansas, our horizons were expanded far beyond Westwood.

From: Norma Jean Taylor Donnell

The treaty of May 10, 1854 between the United States and the Shawnee Tribe of Indians gave the tract of land to Joseph Park. (Seal) President: James Buchanan; Secretary of Interior, J.B. Leonard; Acting Recorder of the General Land Office, Joseph S. Wilson.

Seventy-four years later, on March 23rd, 1928, my father, William F. Taylor and mother Marie G. Taylor paid $300.00 to Carrie S. Garret for Lot 19 in Westport Annex, an addition in Johnson County, Kansas, a lot in the above tract. The transaction went through the Hedrick Abstract and Guaranty Company. The address now is 2012 West 47th Terrace, Westwood, Kansas 66205.

The William Taylor home

My father then started to build our house. He and his brother, Lamonda Taylor, dug out the basement with shovels. My father somehow built the house before my brother, William F. Taylor, Jr. was born in July. Mom said she held a lantern at night so Dad could continue working on the house before my brother was born. He got it done but my aunt Pearl Engle had to hang curtains while Mom was in the hospital giving birth to my brother.

Mom delivered four babies, my brother Bill, myself (Norma Jean), Dolores, and Ronald. We all lived in the two-bedroom house during the Depression and until we were married.

Needless to say, my dad's occupation was carpenter, painter and paper-hanger.

Upon the death of my husband, I

moved back into the empty house the Summer of 1980. My folks had bought and remodeled a home down the street at 1916 W. 47th Terrace. Dad died June 18, 1990, one day after his 91st birthday, and mom died January 17, 1992 at the age of 92.

I still live in the house my father built!

Norma Jean Taylor Donnell

WESTWOOD'S 50TH ANNIVERSARY

From: Betty J. Nourse

Time, and how it has changed Westwood. My husband and I wanted to locate close to our parents, who were "up in years." We also wanted our children to be educated in the Shawnee Mission School District so in 1958 we bought our house on 48th Terrace.

There was the nicest grocery store down on the corner of Rainbow and 48th Terrace. It was so nice to send one of our children to the store, which was "Monteil's" and was also one of the first "super" markets.

On up the street, a block north, where the Rainbow Shops are located, was the wonderful "George Keller's Nursery". On north to 47th and Rainbow, where our beautiful City Hall is located, was a "gas station."

On to the south where Sprint is located, was a row of shops, which included a beauty shop (which is now known as Fairway Beauty Salon, a barber shop, and other stores). There was also a little restaurant, "Ragans," and to the back of the shopping area, an A&P store. On the corner of Belinder and Shawnee Mission Parkway was a furniture store called "Cousins."

As I look back, it really seems like a dream now. But it was all changes known as "progress." All the changes in Westwood, (and there are many more I have not mentioned) it have been changes for the better.

Many people I know here in Westwood have lived in their homes many years. I am glad to see so many new families - young families - moving into homes where the former residents have either moved away to retirement homes or are deceased. That makes it a "new, younger" Westwood, a great place to live and raise a family.

I want to wish Westwood a "Happy 50th Anniversary." I am so happy to have lived in this wonderful community 40 years.

Betty J. Nourse
2326 W. 48th Terrace
Westwood, Kansas 66205

REMEMBRANCES OF WESTWOOD
by Marjorie Thies Jett (written in 1985)

My birth took place on a hot summer day, August 31, 1921. I was the third daughter born to Alfred Charles and Fay Mildred Thies. My two sisters are Virginia Maribelle, born November 28, 1912, and Mary Mildred, born December 12, 1916. At the time of my birth the family lived at 4705 Booth in Johnson County, Kansas. My birth took place in that house. It was considered Kansas City, Kansas, then but is now called Westwood, Kansas.

At any rate, my mother related the story many times concerning my birth. When she felt the time for the delivery was nearing the doctor had come and was waiting downstairs. It was nearing four o'clock in the afternoon and my father was out in the small barn at the end of the back yard milking the cows. My grandmother was in the kitchen cooking a meal so the doctor could have dinner if he had to wait awhile. The doctor went up to check on mother and suddenly the baby came. She and the doctor were alone and when my grandmother came upstairs the doctor, Dr. Berry, had all under control and mother and baby were doing fine. Years later I found the check which must have paid for my birth. It was for $40.

I always understood that my father was disappointed when he learned he had a third daughter. However, I never did feel that he always treated me just like the other two. He never taught any of us to milk the cows, and we had them until I was nearly a teenager.

The house in which I was born had been built by Alfred and Faye about a year after their marriage in 1911. It was on property that adjoined the property and home of my grandparents. In 1901 Thomas Wilson James and his wife Barbara Ann had given a parcel of land there to their daughter, Ida Belle (my grandmother). She and her husband had built a home and moved out from Kansas City, Missouri, about 1902 when my mother was about eleven years old. This is where she grew up along with her brother Henry and sister Ruth. My father and mother bought a piece of that

"DOWNHOME" by Jo Dunham 1982

In September [28] 1861, Ida Belle James was born to Thomas and Barbara Ann (Barrow) James, in Johnson County, Kansas. In 1901, the James gave their daughter a parcel of land at 47th and Hudson Road (now Rainbow Blvd.) [also] in Johnson County. Ida Belle by this time was married to Charles H. Ackerman & their family numbered three children, Henry, Faye & Ruth. Charles & Ida built this house [in 1901] for their family [Henry was 12, Faye was 9 & Ruth was 4]. As the years went by, this house was a very important place for the next two generations of this family. It saw two World Wars, one Great Depression & the effects of such occurences upon a family. It waw the joys & sorrows, the achievements & disappointments, the marriages, births, deaths of family members — all of the events that take place in the history of a family.

In 1979, when the house was no longer occupied by any of the family, it was torn down.

property in 1910. It had been divided into lots by my grand parents. They paid $750 for 3 big lots.

I started life then surrounded by family and was to know it that way all of my growing up years.

It was a wonderful childhood, our home right on the edge of town with us being self sufficient partially for a long time. My father kept milk cows for a long time and there were chickens "downhome," grandma's house. We had a big garden, cherry trees, and raspberry bushes. I took for granted all of those delectable and very fresh foods for all of those years. Besides, we had space.

I was always afraid to reach under those old hens to get the eggs like my grandmother did, but I remember all of the precious little chicks that hatched in spring and I fed the chickens with feed kept in a barrel in the barn lots of times.

My grandfather died when I was about a year old and my Uncle Henry and his wife, Marianna, lived with my grandmother in the gray house. The children born to them: Thomas James, 1924; Alice Marea, 1926; and, Barbara Ann, 1928. Aunt Ruth came back home to live about 1929 or 1930 with her daughter, Maribelle, who was born in 1917. So we were all there - five adults and seven children.

We had plenty of space to play, lots of good food, adults to look after us, and we children did not know there was not much money. My cousins seemed like sisters and a brother.

Some of my early recollections are of spraining my collar bone when being let down suddenly on the teeter totter at my own 6th birthday party. I started to school in a few days and having an injured arm did not help for a good start for a shy and frightened first grader as the old Hudson school at 48th Street right off

Marjorie Thies Jett's grade school photo. Marjorie is second from the left, third row Westwood View School, 3rd & 4th grades

Hudson Road (now Rainbow Blvd.) in Westwood. I soon loved school and often lead my class of about ten students. We had two grades in a room at Hudson and later at the new Westwood School all of my elementary school years. Westwood School was built on 50th Street between Belinder and Rainbow. It was a long walk to school every day up Belinder Road and we were always cautioned not to "cut through" the pasture where there were cattle and perhaps a bull who would chase us, they said, particularly if we happened to be wearing red. We made the walks four times a day because we came home to lunch. We did not walk up and down Hudson Road much (same distance) because the "kids" who walked that route were rather mean or easily provoked and almost daily threatened to "beat up" someone for the slightest happening at school that was displeasing to them. There was a settlement of central European immigrants in an area off Hudson Road and now I know that these bold threats were a defense in a country new to their families. I know they had less that I did and that was very little. Many of my classmates were these children and I'm sure they have grown up to be good citizens - most were very apt students.

I graduated from the eighth grade at Westwood School in a class of twelve in 1935. I was valedictorian of my class and consequently had to give a speech. I wore a white organdy long dress - shirt waist with rhinestone buttons and a peter pan collar. I think this lovely dress cost five dollars, though it may have been fifteen.

Marjorie (Thies) Jett, holding Kenneth Sherrer Jr., summer 1938. Photo taken from back yard of 4705 Booth, where Marjorie grew up. Behind her is old cow barn (on 4705 Booth lot), as her father had 6-8 cows in the 1920's & early 1930's. Behind is roof 4704 Adams chicken house (roosting section) & portion of auto garage for 4704 Adams (with window).

At home during these years, we continued our secure life as children not knowing our parents were going through the great depression. My mother, grandmother, Aunt Marianna, and Aunt Ruth canned great amounts of fruit and vegetables from crates of pineapple and bushels of peaches and crates of plum to green beans, tomatoes, tomato juice. My dad milked twice a day and we had a little milk business - my mother washed all of the bottles and we had a milk route of about 20 customers in the neighborhood and as we grew up we had to help with the delivery. In fact, when I was fourteen my father taught me to drive the car as we delivered the milk - lots of stops and starts so I soon was a master of that gear and letting the clutch out smoothly.

In winter mother, Grammie, and Aunt Marianna would quilt several quilts. They put them in the frames downhome and would quilt day by day till they were finished. When we were very little, before school years, we would play house under the frame while they worked.

Aunt Marianna and Grammie sewed most of our clothes from remnants bought half price at John Taylor's Dry Goods Company downtown in Kansas City, Missouri. Every Friday was remnant day and mother and Aunt Marianna went to shop. I have had many a little dress of a ten cent remnants of cloths.

All of the adults worked very hard during those years to live and give us the great security and foundation that has made all of we seven strong people emotionally, mentally, and physically strong all of our lives so far.

In summer we played fun games in the evenings in the yard - hide and seek, statue, hop scotch, tag. We would very often sit in the big white swing in the yard with our grandmother and she would tell us stories of times when she was little, which was during the civil war.

Our holidays were wonderful, but I will deal with that in another chapter.

One of the chores we children could do was to take the wagon (our child's wagon) and go down to the corner of 47th and Rainbow, one block, to get the ice for the ice box. We could buy the block in 25 pounds for ten cents, 50 pounds for 25 cents, and 100 pounds for 35 cents. I think we usually got 50 pounds and I'm not sure if that would last one day or two. Every lady had ice thongs in their household too. I'm not sure how the ice got from the wagon to the ice box because it was heavy but as the small ice house were we bought it the attendant loaded it and then we would pull the wagon up the slight hill.

Another memory I have of those childhood years - a telephone was not a luxury shared by everyone and we had a phone at our house. Downhome (my grandmother's) they had no phone therefore anyone wanting to reach those who lived down there would call our house. In summer it was easy for we could just go out on the back porch and shout and someone would usually hear us and "whoever" could come to the phone. In winter we usually had to go through the two back yards to get the wanted party. Sometimes though, we could make them hear our shouts through the closed doors.

We also make homemade ice cream frequently with all of those cows (my dad usually had about eight) and when we did both houses had ice cream for their dessert after a meal which was almost twice a week in summer.

I remember the first time we got a refrigerator - it was a unit that fits into our wooden ice box and had a big machine in the basement with tubes

THE ACKERMAN COUSINS

The 7 were grandchildren of Ida Bell (James) Ackerman, (seated, with great-grandson Kenneth Scherrer, Jr. on her lap). Standing left to right: Alice Ackerman Stedman, Barbara Ackerman Fadler, Maribelle McClelland Waid, Virginia Thies Scherrer, Marjorie Thies Jett, Mary Thies Jewell (deceased Aug. 1987, age 72), Thomas J. Ackerman.

The date of the photo is uncertain, K. Scherrer Jr. was born Feb. 24, 1938 & looks about 2 1/2 yrs. old. This would put the date at about 1940. I could have been in conjunction with Mary's wedding on Aug. 25, 1940. Barbara would have been a few days short of 12, Allice 14 1/2 & Tom at just over 16.

Taken on the front porch of the house that was at 4704 Adams St., Johnson County, Kansas, Built in 1901, demolished in 1980

through the floor to make it work. The first night was almost like Christmas for we put water in the pans to make ice and I could scarcely to sleep. I was so anxious to have morning come to see if that water had frozen into ice cubes. Sure enough, it had!

Really, we children grew up in two houses for we were equally comfortable eating or sleeping at either place and there was never such a thing as a baby sitter because some adult was always at home one place or the other to care for us.

When I was about ten a Campfire Girls group was established at our school. Of course, I joined and participated in many fun activities. It gave us a chance to do some of the things the children in the Kansas City, Missouri, schools did. We toured some city businesses, went to the art galleries, etc. In summer, a day camp was held at Swope Park (the big Kansas City park) and several of we little girls would get on the bus near us and then transfer to street cars for a long ride to the park for that day's event. I went many times, whereas today no one would think of letting little girls go that far on public transportation. It was a fairly safe world when I grew up. The ride on public transportation was ten cents.

The Campfire Girl organization also had a week long camp at Late Latawana - an outlying resort area. The fee was $7.00 for the week including everything and I wanted to go so badly but the cost was too great and so I had to suppress that wish.

WHY THE CULLIVANS MOVED TO WESTWOOD

Frank Cullivan gave neighborhood kids many thrills with rides on the small train in his backyaard. Casey Jones didn't have anything on Cullivan when it came to making trains fun!

From: Frank and Maggie Cullivan

In 1947 we were living on the East side of Kansas City, Missouri, and we were looking for a place to buy a house. We heard of a builder who was building houses in the Fromholtz Addition of the Westwood area. We bought the lot on 48th Street and Frank Kraft started on our home in March of 1947. He built several houses on 48th Street. We moved into our home in October of 1947. Our son, John, was born in June of 1948 and our daughter, Coleen, was born in 1953. We needed more space so we added another bedroom and a family room in 1954. We enlarged our kitchen in 1962. We decided to stay in Westwood.

Both of our children went to Roseland School, Old Mission Junior High School and Shawnee Mission North High School. We have been members of Westwood Christian Church since 1950 and are still active members.

We have enjoyed living here and have seen many changes. We remember the "little City Hall" on the corner of 47th and Mission Road, next to the lumber yard. We remember the hardware store, Cousin's Furniture Store, Allens and Kings Drive-ins, all on Johnson Drive, now Shawnee Mission Parkway.

We have enjoyed working with the City Officials and all of the people who have served Westwood at the City Hall.

This is a wonderful city and we recommend it highly.

Frank and Maggie Cullivan

From: Pauline Laird Dykman

I have many fond memories of my childhood in Westwood but I'd like to share one with you that certainly tells you how times have changed in 75 years.

Even though I was a very small child, I remember there was a grocery store on the northeast corner of 47th Terrace and Rainbow, known as Wrightsman's Grocery Store.

Several mornings a week, early in the morning, Buddy Wrightman (son of owner) came to our home to take our grocery order, writing it on a pad and telling my Mother what the good specials were. He went to many houses in the neighborhood as few families had telephones to call in their grocery orders. In the afternoon, he delivered our grocery order and my Mother signed the bill.

My father stopped at the store on Saturday and paid for the week's groceries and received a brown sack filled with penny candies in gratitude for prompt payment. My sister, Elma Louise, and I, eagerly awaited our Father's arrival knowing he would have that bag of candy. We greeted him with great affection, trading hugs and kisses for that bag of goodies. In 1924, at the age of six months. my parents (Elmer and May Laird) bought a home in Mission Township (later Westwood) where I resided until 1947, when I married Leroy Dykman. We moved into an apartment across the street while we were building our first home on a vacant lot next to my parent's home. We lived there with our two sons, Steve and Gary, until 1987, when we built our present home on 48th Terrace in Westwood Hills.

Even though I moved to Westwood Hills, I still feel physically close to Westwood as our backyard fence is on the border dividing Westwood and Westwood Hills.

I have many fond memories of growing up in Westwood, attending Westwood View School, Shawnee Mission Rural High School and raising our two sons, Steve and Gary, and attending their graduations from Westwood View and Shawnee Mission North High School. Two of our four grandchildren attend Westwood View School. I am proud to have been a Westwood citizen for 63 years and have watched its development and progress during this time. From a small area in the most northeast corner of Johnson County, Westwood has grown to be a beautiful little city. I have listed just a few improvements through the years: Became an incorporated city, installed a sewer system, hard surfaced streets, curbs and gutters, sidewalks and street lights, changed to Johnson County Water District #1, built a new grade school, built a new City Hall, improved fire and police protection and citizens have access to a beautiful racquet club and swimming pools. We are now living in Westwood Hills and involved with our city's 50th anniversary celebration but plan to celebrate with Westwood, too.

Pauline Laird Dykman

WESTPORT ANNEX WATER COMPANY HISTORY

From: Leroy A. Dykman

This Water Company was chartered November 23, 1923, and was liquidated December 31, 1988 after 65 years. The area includes 47th Terrace, 48th Street, North side 48th Terrace, from Rainbow to State Line, and both sides of Rainbow from 47th Terrace to 48th Terrace. It consisted of 103 customers.

Water lines were laid by the property owners. Each property had a meter in the basement or in the meter pit. A seven member board of directors was elected each year at their annual meeting. Bob Cline was President and Leroy Dykman was Secretary - Treasurer, with the help of his wife, Pauline, for the last 34 years.

This Water Company was dissolved on December 31, 1988, and taken over by Water District No. 1 of Johnson County, Kansas.

From: Elizabeth Sorenson

It happened the day before Thanksgiving, November in 1963: A huge moving van moved slowly down Belinder Court, stopping at 4843, and prepared to unload its cargo there.

Thanksgiving Day came with the new day, but with piled up boxes, furniture, etc., there was little to remind you it was the traditional turkey day. Dinner didn't resemble the first Thanksgiving so many, many years before, but McDonald's had plenty of french fries, luscious hamburgers and hot coffee, so the first Thanksgiving dinner in my new home was really a happy one.

The Saturday that followed set the pattern for the days that followed: Neighbors, Lois Nohe, Anne Wolfe and Faye Hudam, called and officially welcomed me to the neighborhood. Others followed and it wasn't long before still others made me welcome.

In the years that have followed it has been a real pleasure to see a small section of the city build itself with the many things that made a city, and do it without argument, but with community meetings and discussions. So, the old school was torn down; A new, enlarged building emerged, with a park close by.

The council met in various places including the building that has just now been slated for remodeling. It was here the subject of whether to sell the large plot of land for a radio station came to the front. That, too, was approved, but the people wisely decided that, if in the future the radio station closed up, Westwood would have the first refusal to buy back their land.

There have been many improvements made in the years that have followed: The handsome City Hall, and improvements too numerous to mention, but the important things to remember are that each and every improvement was done with the approval of its citizens, without disagreement, or argument; and Westwood has become the neatest small city, both near and far. We have been so fortunate in leaders, who seem to be continually on the watch for ways to improve the city.

I could go on for a long time recounting the many things experienced in the small section in which I live, including doing social things together, and I really think it is true of others as well. Soon we will be turning the calendar to January 1, 2000, and it is "Best Wishes for the future, to the best little city in Kansas," and a personal wish from me, that this will always be my home.

Elizabeth Sorenson

MY MEMORIES BEFORE WESTWOOD CITY

From: Marie Stockhbauer

When I was nine years old, my parents bought a four-room house and property on 47th Terrace which later they remolded. The house is still there.

All the children in the neighborhood attended Hudson School - about 1/2 block from Hudson Road. Hudson Road is now Rainbow Blvd. Hudson School was a four-room school. My teacher's name was Mrs. Odom. At that time there were two classes in one room. Mrs. Odom taught both classes. Our principal's name was Mr. Christy. When the classes graduated from Hudson School they attended Shawnee Mission Rural High School, which now is Shawnee Mission North. The students had to walk to 47th and Mission Road to ride on the Strang Line to school.

On the south corner of 47th Terrace and Hudson Road was a grocery store that was owned by Mrs. Carter. She later built a new store and an apartment beside it as her home, where the Pride Cleaners and Alberti Gunter are located now. After her death Wayne Wrightsman and Bud Smith became the new grocery store men. One day a robber entered the store and Mr. Wrightsman was shot. It left him with a limp.

Some other business places were Mr. Glazer and Sons furnace company, and a riding academy owned by Mr. Horner as well as a driving tee for golfers in the area of the KMBC tower.

Marie Stockhbauer

The entire student body of Hudson School. Year of this photo is unknown, but Hudson closed in 1928

From: Lyle Wrightman

I am 66 years old and have spent most of my life living in the City of Westood, except for a brief period when I lived one and one half blocks out of Westwood. I have since been living at 2905 W. 50th Place since 1963.

As a small boy I remembered Rainbow Blvd. was called Hudson Road, a two-lane covered with brick and black top having no curbs or gutters. It ran from 47th Street to Shawnee Mission Parkway
known as 50 Highway.

There was a Shell Service Station located on the northwest corner and later became a Mobil Station and remained until Telecommunication Complex (now Sprint) was built.

My father own land on the east side of Rainbow and 47th Terrace. He opened a grocery store there named HGF Grocer. This was the only grocery store in Westwood at that time.

Where the shopping center is now located between 47th Terrace and 48thTerrace was vacate land. Several of my relatives owned several areas in the city. Two homes were located west on 47th Terrace and one home south on Rainbow were owned by relatives. Later the Rainbow Nursery, owned by George Keller, occupied the North edge of 47th Terrace. In one of the houses south of the Nursery, the Keller family lived.

The last large plot of land, owned by my Grandparents, and located west of Belinder between 50th Terrace and 51st Street was sold and several homes now occupy that area.

I attended kindergarten at Westwood View School and I graduated from the eighth grade in 1946. I believe the picture of our class is still hanging in the hallway.

In the late 30s or probably in 1940 a large rain storm came in with terrific winds and blew down the KMBZ radio tower, nearly splitting a house located on Booth Street in two. I rode my bicycle up to see the damage. I also recall the construction of homes being built on Adams Street while walking to school. My youngest son lives in one of those homes at the present.

The area located on the 47th and Mission Road corner had the small city hall, a Phillips 66 Service Station which was owned by the Schleicher Family. A grease rack located in the back of station had only one bay for service. There was barber shop, small auto repair garage, nursery owned by Peter Martin and Logan Moore Lumber Yard.

Across 47th Street out of Westwood was a two-story brick building. It was used as a printing shop for several years, but later was used as church and school. It was the first St. Agnes School and Church. The first floor was the school and second floor the church. This was used until the present church was built on the Southwest corner of Mission Road. I knew several children that attended the school.

Lyle Wrightman

KANSAS
RETAIL CIGARETTE LICENSE
1951
№ 137

To Whom it May Concern:

BE IT KNOWN, That........Elizabeth C. Wrightsman........,
(Owner, individual name; if partnership, co-partner's names; if corporation, corporate name)

doing business as........Waynes Market........, having made application and paid
(Trade name)

$5.00 license fee as required by law, is hereby LICENSED AS A RETAIL DEALER IN CIGARETTES to conduct a retail cigarette business at........4755 Rainbow........Kansas City........being the
(Street and number, R. F. D.)   (City or town)
exact location where cigarettes are sold under this license, subject to the restrictions and requirements of the laws of the State of Kansas, and the rules and regulations of the Director of Revenue, State Commission of Revenue and Taxation.

This license shall be in force and effect on and after........January 1........, 1951, to and including December 31, 1951.

IN WITNESS WHEREOF, I have hereunto set my hand at Topeka, Kansas,

this....5th....day of....December........, 195 0

........BERT E. MITCHNER, Director of Revenue.

This License Shall be Kept Posted in a Conspicuous Place Where Sales are Made

23-5347-s   9-50—15,000   FORM C-157

A state license was required to sell cigarettes at the HGF Grocer, Westwood's only grocery store in 1950.

From: Cecil and Hazel Waage

Our family moved to Westwood in the fall of 1956. At the time we moved we didn't fully realize the many advantages Westwood offered, the quiet, safe neighborhood with its tree lined streets was a great place to raise three children.

The Westwood View School is still one of the finest schools in Johnson County. We remember the old school building which was razed in 1968 to make way for the present school. We also remember the city hall being in a small building on what is now the IGA grocery parking lot at 47th and Mission Road.

Westwood has been blessed over the years with a fine city government and an excellent police department, although both were much smaller in the fifties and sixties.

We remember the old Phillips Gas Station at the site of our present City Hall at 47th and Rainbow. We remember the old Montiel's grocery store at 48th and Rainbow.

We also remember the small farm with a cow that existed until the early sixties on the west side of Belinder Street at 50th Terrace. Later most of the streets in the neighborhood were widened and recurbed as the city prospered in the seventies.

Some of the city prosperity came about when the Sprint Company (formerly United Utilities) came to the city and expanded the old Hallmark site on Shawnee Mission Parkway. We remember the former businesses that existed on the Sprint complex site, the A&P Grocery, Dorothy Rose Beauty Shop, Hudson Gas Station and the Barber Shop.

We are proud to be residents of Westwood and hope our association will continue for some years to come.

Cecil and Hazel Waage
2504 W. 50th Place
Our children: Cheryl Waage Miller, Susan Waage Schram and Steven Waage

From: Robert Dye

Rainbow was a brick street from Bell Memorial Hospital (K.U. Medical), to 47th Street. 47th Street was a gravel street west, past a small service station located at what is now Belinder Road. The station was operated by Gaither and Lena (Fromholtz) Myers, friends of my parents. I sometimes helped out at the service station.

There were a few homes in the area with fruit trees, gardens, and a milk cow now and then. This was Westwood in the early 30s. I was in the area only occasionally in the 40s.

After serving in World War II and the Korean conflict, I returned in 1951 with my bride, Lorraine, to a new home at 4718 Booth. A few years and two children later (Bob & Beverly), we built our present home at 4701 Booth, in 1959.

The following years we saw many changes in Westwood. 47th Street was a narrow lane changed to a four lane curbed street. In the 50s I worked on the construction of a new building on Shawnee Mission Parkway known as the Hallmark Building (now part of Sprint), and also a new building on Rainbow, The Hudson building.

In the 80s I retired from construction and took an interest in City Government. After searching the area and considering various possibilities, we agreed on a location for our present City Hall at 47th and Rainbow. I was very proud when Mayor Kostar asked me to preside at the dedication of the new City Hall. What a great day ! Thanks to all who made it possible. We can all be proud of our City, our beautiful city hall, and the accomplishments of our city officials, past and present. Their plans were on target, and our present officials are doing what it takes to keep our city as popular as it is. Keep up the good work.

From left to right: Temporary Barracks, Hinch Hall, and Bell Memorial Hospital (present day KU Medical Center), circa 1930. *Photo courtesy the University of Kansas Medical Center Archives, Department of History and Philosophy of Medicine.*

Hope Westwood has another 50 years of prosperity.

Robert Dye

From: The Morris Riggs Family

The Riggs Family moved from Sedalia, Missouri in 1919.

There was five boys and five girls in the family. George and his wife settled at 4519 State Line then called the Westport area.

Three of the brothers were engineers and worked for the Frisco railroads. The other two worked for the postal service.

One of the girls named Annie Riggs married a Mr. Hill and she is still living on 46th. and Francis Street in Wyandotte County of Kansas City, Kansas. She still plays the organ and piano for her church, the Espworth Methodist Church located on the NE corner of Genesee Street.

Morris Riggs was born May 1921 at the home, 4608 Eaton in Kansas city, Kansas. The family moved several time and even moved into Westwood at the house located at 50th. Street and Rainbow just south of the Swatzell property. He and Jack Swatzell became very good friends. They seemed to get in a lot of trouble especially at school. They attended Westwood View when Mr. Fordyth was the principal. Several spanking were given to straightened them out. He always enjoyed going over to Jack home for his mother Bertie always had the cookie jar ready for the boys. They played in the tower yard of KMBC Radio station, the Green Parrot Restaurant, and the little branch creek located in Westwood Hills.

76

Rainbow was a two lane asphalt road and called Hudson Road. His father, George operated the Phillips 66 station located on the corner of Hudson road and County Line Road (47th. Street), also the garage just west of the station in the late 30's. Along that area was a barber shop called Pat's Barber Shop and a small Hamburger cafe.

State Line road was a very narrow road with the trolley rails down the center which made it very hard for vehicles to pass. The trolley went south on State Line from 39th. Street and was called the Sunset Line to 45th. Because of the size of the trolley it had to make a 90° arch which ran up to Bell Street to be able to turn around for the trip back north. The name of Roanoke 45 was given to part of the line. People waiting to take the trolley usually waited in the Schuler drug Store or the Hamburger Cafe. Other small businesses were located there. Morris stated boys would be boys and would try to jump on the trolley to get a free ride. Naturally they were made to get off.

Morris still visits in Westwood area especially visiting with his friend, Jim Hayner (the City of Westwood Building Inspector). They were pilots in World War II and became good friends. Morris spends a lot of time on his lake property in the Ozarks.

From: Janet Hosty

We moved to Westwood on January 15, 1966.

Our interests have always been church, school and community and they still are.

We registered at St. Agnes parish and enrolled five of our nine children in St. Agnes. As we became involved in the parish and community, we became aware of the need for a bond issue to rebuild Westwood View School. We had always felt that a good public school system was the strength of the community so Jim and I became involved in helping to get the bonds approved for the rebuilding of the school. We were very proud when it passed and the school was rebuilt.

Our son Dick went to Westwood View School and Old Mission. Tom and Kathy attended kindergarten at Westwood View. I was active in the PTO and was on the board when the exercise trail was built in cooperation with the City of Westwood.

During the years we lived in Westwood, I served on the following boards: St. Agnes School Board, Westwood View PTO, Old Mission PTO, Bishop Miege Parents Representative Board, Shawnee Mission Chapter Red Cross. While on City Council, I was proud to be a part of the purchase and renovation of the Public Works building under the direction of Gene Culbertson.

While I served as Parks and Recreation Chairman, the Summer Intern Program hired a student from a university to provide recreation programs for Westwood citizens from childhood pre-school to senior. Some of the programs were the annual 4th of July Celebration, and the concert in the Park. Farewell to Summer Concert in the Park with the Big Band Sound and dancing around the fountain. Will anyone forget Walt Tylickis enjoying every last dance of summer? What about the ice cream social? I'll bet only a handful will remember the first and only watermelon social. Joe Dennis, our then Mayor donated the watermelons. If you don't remember don't worry, we were only a few in number but we had fun.

During this time we purchased the land and created the little mini park next to the animal hospital. In the Westwood tradition of a beautiful little city, the public works building was landscaped and park benches added as another little mini park.

Truly the most exciting and satisfying experience was the opportunity I had to serve on the committee to plan and build the new City Hall. The most satisfaction comes from hearing how much it is used. The whole purpose was to have our own gathering place and to serve our wonderful Police Department with a safe and secure facility.

Ten years ago Westwood was planning it's 40th Anniversary and I was on that committee. The present yearly calendar format was created for the 40th Anniversary year. It was a good beginning and the last decade has been even better for Westwood. We broke ground for City Hall ten years ago and it has become a beacon for Westwood as one enters the City, "The greatest little City in the World!!!!!"

From: Nancy Jeffries

Jeff and I bought our very first home, 4831 Booth in Westwood, in May, 1963. We lived there until 1980, when we purchased 4815 Belinder and lived there until 1985 when we were transferred to Morris, Illinois, by Jeff's job.

I was always interested in government and in 1970 I decided to "test the waters" and filed to run for City Council. Boy, was I naive, I filed quite early and it must have scared the men so badly that before I knew it nine men filed to run.

I'm sure some of them were recruited to break up the vote. One of them distributed a flyer stating "No Gripes, No Grudges, No promises, No Platform." Well, I lost the election, but I sure learned plenty. By 1972, I had become better known and had organized my campaign, plus there was internal feuding on the Council. That caused the defeat of two incumbents and my election. That really caused an uproar. A watering can with flowers was delivered to the Westwood Police Dept. from Roeland Park's Police Department as a sign of sympathy. It seems funny now, but we have to remember that back then women in elective offices were very few and far between. I was almost a pioneer. It just meant I had to study harder and work more hours to prove I could be effective and, I think I was!

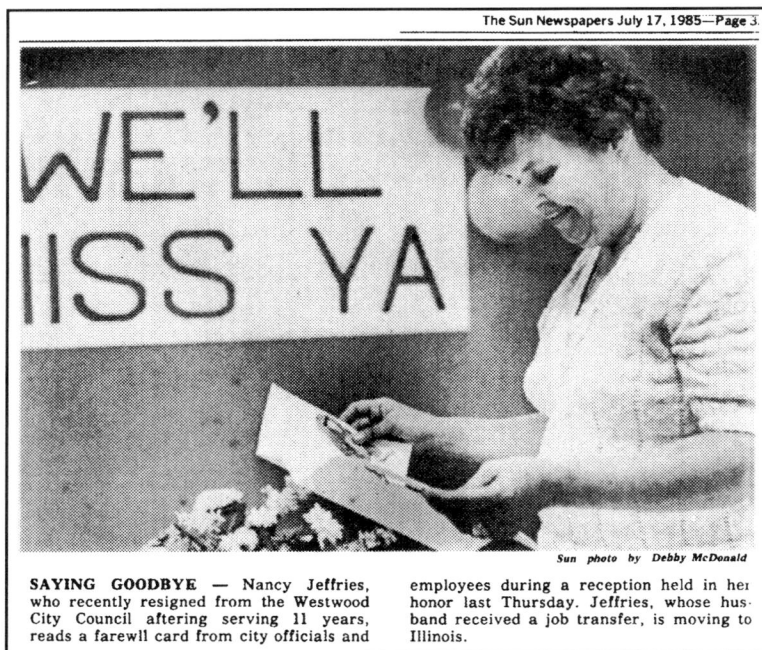

The Sun Newspapers July 17, 1985—Page 3.

SAYING GOODBYE — Nancy Jeffries, who recently resigned from the Westwood City Council aftering serving 11 years, reads a farewll card from city officials and employees during a reception held in her honor last Thursday. Jeffries, whose husband received a job transfer, is moving to Illinois.

Nancy Jeffries became Westwood's first female city council member in 1973. She served 11 years before her husband was transferred to a job in Illinois.

The things I am most proud of, that I accomplished while on the Council were the establishment of our Annual Tree Planting Program city wide, the development of the park at 50th and Rainbow, and the additional beautification projects through out the city.

I also proposed and directed the City Celebration of the 25th Anniversary of incorporation, with lots of help from Chief Al Wrinkle. We had a Miss Westwood Contest, a big parade and all kinds of activities for a whole weekend.

Another thing I got started was the Annual Westwood Night at the Ball Park. The first year we did it the game was at the old Municipal Stadium. The next year, we went to the new Royal's Stadium. In all the years we held this event, we only had one rain out.

There are a million fond memories of my life as a council member, and stories galore, but not for publication. Just know that we think of Westwood often and miss all of our friends and neighbors.

WHY WE CHOSE WESTWOOD – AND STAYED

From: Allene and Bill Plant

It was 1965, we were expecting our first child and in the market for our first home. The search extended from County Line to 95th Street, State Line to Nall and included Fairway, Prairie Village, Overland Park, Westwood Hills and Westwood. We looked at a lot of houses.

Our first priority was an excellent elementary school that would be close, for we only anticipated being in the area for some seven years or so. Westwood View filled the elementary school requirement and Old Mission and Shawnee Mission North completed our daughter's education. As with most couples seeking their first home, cost is also a major factor. The cost of a typical Westwood house in the mid-1960s was within our price range; a figure quite different from the numbers we see today, approximately $18,000.00. Thirty-four years later we're still here.

The image we see of Westwood has changed drastically during these three and half decades. The area around Woodside was a 17-acre, highly eroded piece of bare land. IGA occupies a site of a former lumberyard. Westwood did have an abundance of service stations as Mobil, Phillips, Skelly, Texaco and Amaco were all present. The Sprint World Headquarters was a Hallmark building and a strip shopping center, featuring an A & P grocery. The Intercom broadcasting facility was merely a transmitter site, completely fenced with chain link. The Westwood Village shopping center was a nursery. The Westwood Park at 50th and Rainbow was the location of two houses and a small orchard.

The services offered by the City of Westwood were far different than those provided today. One police car, no leaf pick-up, street cleaning consisting of a jeep and a trailer, naturally no recycling or composting program and a street improvement program that was hardly more than a dream.

While the city has certainly changed, one thing has remained constant, that being a small town atmosphere in an urban setting. The warm, friendly greetings of neighbors, the services provided by the city and the continuous improvement of individual properties all contribute to making Westwood a great place to live.

We're glad we stayed.

Allene and Bill Plant

From: Claude Percy

Yvonne and I moved our family to Westwood in 1964, lured by the school and the wonderful appearance of the neighborhood. Our particular neighborhood consisted of young families with a gazzillion children, and several of the original residents who had built their houses in the late thirties and early forties. This mix of ages made for a rich experience for all of us.

One of the earliest civic events I remember attending was the annual school board election at Westwood View. This was an old fashioned town hall type meeting where everyone was asked to step up and give their expectations for our schools. I was overwhelmed by the civility shown to everyone that participated. We decided then and there this was the right place for us. Since that time property values have soared, the appearance of the town has blossomed, and we have attracted new, involved citizens.

I bought my house from Bill Weeks, one of the early mayors of Westwood. He told me one of the biggest budget decisions one year was whether to put two new tires on the police car, or a complete set of retreads. Today we have these great little parks, our leaves are picked up for us each fall, streets are being paved each year, our police department is second to none, and our City tax levy is not as high as it was in 1964. Things have certainly changed. One that hasn't changed though is you can still call your council representative or the mayor and get an attentive ear.

Living in a beautiful little town, close to the cultural centers of the metropolitan area, is a real plus. The greatest plus though is living in a community of neighbors who know and care for one another. I think we have something here that will last another 50 years. We must be doing something right because of the number of second and third generation Westwood residents buying homes and raising families here!

Westwood 50th Anniversary Celebration
1949 to 1999
by Claude Percy

From: Dave Buck

50 Years of Westwood History: We Bucks have been Westwood residents for the last 10(+-) years, so I can comment only on the last decade. The following is our family's history in Westwood.

When my wife and I started looking for our first home, we looked everywhere in the Metro area. We mutually decided that we should focus on one area, Westwood, Kansas. At this point in time, I can't tell you one particular reason why we made that decision but will definitely say it was the right one. Realtors always say "location, location, location", but Westwood offers much more.

We bought our first house at 4919 Adams. As I said before, I do not remember why we decided Westwood, but I hope this story will help explain why we have stayed. We moved ourselves from a rental property between Westport and the Plaza. We had agreed to purchase our new house a few weeks beforehand, but unfortunately the previous owner had not been too vigilant with yard maintenance between then and closing. As we approached with our first pick-up load, the immediate thing I noticed was a knee deep front lawn. This being our first house, we had yet to purchase a lawn mower. Our move also happened to coincide with the weekend my sister had organized a surprise birthday party for my mom in Wichita. We hauled as much as we could that day before heading "home" to the birthday party. We came back the next day to continue the move. When we approached our new house again, with another load of stuff, we were more than pleasantly surprised to find that a wonderful neighbor (thank you Walt) had welcomed us by cutting our yard. That act alone was very telling of what to expect from the neighborhood. It's the people or neighbors who make this place great.

Our first Westwood house was a genuine "fixer-upper". To be honest, our intent was to do just that, fix it up, and move on. Both Donna and I are in the construction field, she's an Architect and I am an Engineer. So, with her design talents and both of our backs, we envisioned about two years of house improvements and then on to something bigger and better. To try and make a long story short, after about nine years of sweat and lots of money, we finally had a home that we could invite over friends and relatives and not be too embarrassed by unfinished projects.

Then we got a dog, Maxine. This acquisition, no regrets on that money well spent, led to many walks through the neighborhood. On one such family outing, we saw our current home at 2332 W. 51st Street. The owner, a previous long time resident of the city, had decided to move closer to her children and was letting her sons handle the sale of 2332, something that was not at the top of their priority list. There was no "For Sale" sign out front, and the house apparently had been unoccupied for a number of months. We were kind of nosey, looked around the exterior, and decided that we wanted to investigate further. Fortunately for us, a friend lived next door and told us whom to contact. Again trying not to be too long winded, we decided to buy the place (justifying the move on a bigger backyard for Max). Somehow, and despite me dragging my feet, we did just that and moved two blocks south of the house we had just spent most of our married lives working on. We are now working on the next "labor of love", our second "money pit" (another fixer-upper).

This piece is to be part of a "50 year" memorial book. During our decade here, there have been lots of different things that have inspired and driven our family's community commitment and involvement. I was asked to give my history of the city, and have written probably more than most wanted to know about us. But, in our brief time here, there have also been numerous changes citywide that have affected everyone. In just the last ten years, a new City Hall has been built, there have been changes in the city staff and elected representatives, businesses and residents have come and gone, the community has reemphasized different community events, the list goes on.

Every city experiences some of the above, but what makes Westwood unique is it is still a thriving, prospering, growing community. In my opinion a "destination" community. I think what continues to be our most compelling city asset is our neighbors, those next door and those two or more blocks away. It was very hard to leave 4919 Adams, but our new location (if/when it gets put into shape) is truly our home. I no longer consider trips to Wichita as going "home", it is the drive back when I'm homeward bound.

Dave Buck
Councilperson, 1995 to present

From: Jim Donovan

"Jim, your mother and I have to sell the house. You need to clean the basement."

Oh, those dreaded words. "Clean the basement." Just the thought of doing so still sends a chill down my spine.

Never mind the fact that I was twenty something years old at the time. The fact remains that my dad was telling me to go clean the basement. Hey, I have two brothers and three sisters. Why do I have to clean the basement?

Lets ignore the fact that all the "kids" have moved out and established their own life. Lets forget the fact that seniority has its privilege and there are three siblings younger than me. Heck, lets even forgo the obvious fact that most everything down there is mine. The bottom line is that dad told me to go clean the basement.

You see, this whole problem started in 1965 when mom and dad were going to put an offer on a house in Prairie Village. They could not get a hold of their agent, however. A chance call to the agent's office resulted in another agent recommending that they go look at a small house in Westwood. Dad drove by it and made an offer without consulting the "boss". I guess everything worked out OK because mom approved.

Well, we all moved into the house. As the story goes, my older sisters and I went to the neighbors house and started to use sticks to splash all the water out of the bird bath. The elderly residents saw us doing so, my big sisters got scarred and ran home (just across the driveway). The owner came out, introduced herself and her husband, and offered me a cookie. I obliged and Dr. and Mrs. Price became good, lifelong friends.

Another good, lifelong friend that we soon met were the Woster's. They lived right behind us over the white picket fence. To this day I can remember my mother holding me in her arms and introducing ourselves to Mrs. Woster. I reached up, slapped the glasses off her face and broke them. First impressions are so very important. I was too young to be embarrassed, although I am sure mom was.

As luck would have it, the neighborhood was full of kids. We soon learned that one new family that moved in across the street came from Prairie Village. As luck would have it, they moved from the same neighborhood that my parents were going to move into. I guess that fate truly is something you can not escape.

Well, the years flew by and a lot of things have changed. I can remember various street projects but remember our street and the Mission Road project vividly. I believe there being so many kids in the neighborhood resulted in a night security guard on the Mission Road project. There were many open man holes to be investigated and quite a bit of wet cement that needed to be written on. Of course, my parents did not raise me to be one of the kids that would write my name in cement, but I did do some investigating.

Another big project was the development of what became Woodside Racket Club. I can recall a petitioner coming around to the house asking for signatures in order to start and complete the project. Once complete, there was the usual childhood bet on who will be the first to jump into the pool. We Donovan's were sure that we would win. Fate, however, thought otherwise. The "new" family from what would have been our other Prairie Village neighbor beat us. Upon reflection, I guess that we were lucky. The water was cold. Fate could have saved us, but I like to think of it as a cruel way of getting even.

Many other things changed throughout the years. Hallmark cards came, the old A&P moved, Sprint came, the neighborhood movie theater closed (no more summer movies on Thursday mornings), and so on. One thing that never seemed to change as a child was the neighbors. Many of my childhood neighbors were the original owners of the property. The Price's built their house in 1936. The Meyer's soon followed. Mrs. Mallot, Mrs. Moidl, they all built their house as did many others that I fail to remember now.

Many other houses are still to this day referred to by the people that lived in the house when I was a kid. The Hosty's, the Kellerman's, the McEnulty's, the Carter's, the other Carter's (no relation, but they did accidentally run into each other at Disneyland on their vacation one year), the purple house (aptly named after the color of the trim and the color of the cap the owner always use to wear), the haunted house (every neighborhood has to have one, its a requirement in every childhood).

The most vivid memory of my childhood is probably the seemingly 50 kids in the neighborhood getting together after dinner to play hide and seek. It was great. We would entertain ourselves for hours. I thought we had the best group and hiding places for miles. The base was always the tree in our front yard and the game would last until 10pm. Then I learned that kids in another neighborhood played the game also, but they thought that theirs was the best game. They lived on a dead end and used the stop sign at the end of the street for base. Their rule was that you had to slap the sign to be "free". I do not know which neighborhood actually had the best game, but I do find it odd that one of the guys that use to slap the sign the hardest is now in charge of replacing the signs that are bent.

Well, lets get back to the problem at hand. "Jim, go clean the basement." I would rather perform my own dental surgery. For the year and a half prior to this command I had been working in Pittsburg, Kansas. To top it off, my bride of 6 months was now by my side.

Well, fate played its fickle hand again. Both my wife and I were offered jobs in the greater Kansas City market place and we decided to relocate. We needed housing and we needed it now. My job was in downtown and hers was in Olathe. Rather than clean the basement, we decided to buy the house (by far the lesser of two evils). My wife and I figured that within two years we will find a house that we like in a neighborhood we like and move.

Well, the two years came and went. We did look for a house and developed a list of what we want in a house and a neighborhood. The problem was that we could not find what we were looking for. We wanted an established neighborhood that did not require a car to get around in and had good schools. The house needed to be so many bedrooms and baths with all the modern-day conveniences - big kitchen, large garage, adequate space, etc. Were we asking for too much?

Honestly speaking, I got fed up with looking. All that various agents and our own efforts landed us with were houses that had all the curb appeal of cold toast. I was so tired of looking for a house that I told Peggy, my wife, that I quite. I would not look at any more houses.

I think Peggy looked for one more weekend and came to the same conclusion. We decided to remodel the house we were in. Well, we started the project just prior to the birth of our oldest almost 8 years ago. Using the equity we built up, we did a second phase in 1998 (we are almost finished with it now). With any luck, we will start our third and final phase soon.

The most important thing that I have observed over the past 35 plus years of being in Westwood is that there are many other second generation families buying their parents house. I would be willing to bet that others find themselves in situations just like ours. They want the best world for themselves and their kids and they found it right where they were all along - Westwood.

Click your heals together three times and say "There's no place like home."

Jim Donovan

OLDER RESIDENTS

Nick Fromholtz: 1897-'98

Nick was 1 1/2 years old when his father bought 5 acres of land. He built a house at 49th and Mission Rd, long known as "Gunther's Place." He planted fruits and vegetables, and a flower garden on the land. The children attended school in K. C. Roe's house, which was east of Mission Building. Water was hauled from Brush Creek in barrels for the livestock. To earn money, the family sold sauerkraut and cottage cheese from house to house by quarts.

Nick served in World War I. When he returned, dairy farms were still around, and Mr. Meekam raised beef cattle. Nick's father was also raising hogs. His father purchased a 1916 Oldsmobile and a one-ton Olds truck.

In 1926 Nick bought a 1923 Willis Knight Sedan, which he used for 10 years. He was married in 1926 to a girl from Louisburg. He built a home at 48th and Mission Road, and 2 1/2 acres came with the purchase. The total cost was $950 for land and house. In 1960- two houses down from corner, on same piece of land. After Second World War, the home was being built and Nick began plotting off lots and selling land.

Mr. and Mrs. Nick Fromholtz

Nick also sold and delivered rice to homes and businesses, then later opened a Norge Store and sold refrigerators, washers, and ironing machines. He lived away from Westwood only for a brief period.

FORMER OFFICIAL SEES CHANGE

Glenn A. Myers has been close to the growth of Westwood as a city in several official capacities.

"I've seen a lot of things change," Myers said recently in a discussion of his involvement in service to the city.

He and his wife moved into their new home at 5105 Mission Road in 1936. In the years since then Myers has served on the Westwood View School Board, as a Westwood city councilman, as the city treasurer, and as financial advisor to the city.

Last January Westwood honored him for his years of service with the presentation of a plaque noting his contributions.

The biggest change Myers has noted in his years in Westwood has been "the filling up of the open spaces. There are no big parcels of land left now within the city, but there were some then (late 30's and early 40's). Where highway 50 runs, much of that was pasture. An elderly lady owned a big piece of land and the city just left it alone as long as she lived. Up until just a few years ago, the Woodside Racquet Club area was just a big pasture."

In 1936 the Myers could look across Mission Road, then an oiled thoroughfare, to a 27 hole golf course. "We thought that golf course would be there forever," Mrs. Myers chuckled. Myers explained, "The land was owned by the Roes. When they died, much of it went to the church." Today it is the site of St. Agnes and Bishop Meige High School.

Myers served on the School Board from 1945 to 1954. "I remember someone called and asked me to serve. He said he'd give me half an hour to consider. I took the half hour and said 'yes,'" It was a three-man school board. The school was the old Westwood View building, "with some additions. I think, in the early 40's." Enrollment, then still through the 8th grade, was about 350.

Myers recalled that the major problem facing the board then was "finding enough money to pay the teachers' salaries. The teachers then made something less than $2,000 a year. But our tax base just wasn't very big."

His time of service with the city government ran from 1961 to 1973, including council terms and serve as city treasurer. And again, he recalls, sufficient funding was a problem. "I can remember an annual city budget of $60,000 to $65,000. Now it's a million dollar budget. The intangibles tax the city receives from the major utility company within the city limits has made that growth possible.

"But I remember trying to find enough money to really build a police department in the early 60's.

"I saw lots of good things happen while I was on the council - free trash pick up for the residents, the expansion of the police department, the growth of City Hall."

For a short time in the early 40's, the Myers lived in Iowa and rented out their home in Westwood. They returned as soon as they could. And, both agree, they want to live nowhere else.

STILL LIVES IN SAME SPOT

Ada Reynolds

In the summer of 1903 Ada (Ketrow) Reynolds moved with her parents and her sister Anna to the part of Westwood that was then called Westport Annex.

She has lived on the original property ever since. Today she lives at 2122 W. 47th Terrace. Her sister, now Mrs. William Laird, and her husband lived just down the street at 2100 W. 47th Terrace.

Now almost 82 years old, Mrs. Reynolds has many vivid memories of the area and its growth into a city. This spring she gathered some of those memories in an essay entitled "Reminiscences." From that essay and a pleasant conversation in her living room emerged the following picture of early Westwood, particularly the Westport Annex area.

"We moved from Kansas City to Westport Annex in July of 1903. With the help of our friends, our father built our home on West 47th Terrace at what is now 2202."

The big two-story frame house still stands, just east of Rainbow. The home Mrs. Reynolds lives in was built later on the original land Mr. Ketrow bought.

"There were no electric lights, gas, city water, or paved streets. We carried water from the spring on the Elmer Swatzell property (a dairy farm) about two blocks away. We used coal-oil lamps, and heated and cooked with wood and coal. What is now Westwood Hills was pasture land for Charles Swatzell (also a dairy farm). There was a creek through it, and the trees along the creek had sturdy grapevines entwined through them. The Annex children, as they swam and played there, would swing across the creek on these vines.

"After several months we had a cistern in our back yard, and later the real estate company had two wells dug to supply the three streets in the Annex, 47th Terrace, 48th Street, and Swatzell Road, from State Line to Hudson Road (now rainbow Avenue).

"We had two lots and our father planted fruit trees, shade trees and grapevines around our two story frame house. At that time there were only a few houses and one grocery store owned and operated by Henry Clayzer.

"My sister and I went through 8th grade at the Mission school. We went to our commencement exercises at Olathe, where all the schools had their ceremonies.

"Then I went to Westport High School in Missouri. I always walked, and I often stopped at my aunt's house along the way to get warm."

Mr. and Mrs. William Laird

What did two young girls in the early 20th century do for recreation? "Well, we did a lot of handwork and both my sister and I always read a lot. We helped mother, we were involved in the church. And then there was a 5-cent movie not far from here. It just seemed there were always lots of things going on."

Mrs. Reynolds commented frequently on the community spirit of the Annex people.

"We didn't have all these improvements then and we really didn't think anything about it. But when the people did want something improved, the men would get out and work on it themselves. Even though they all had regular jobs, they'd use their spare time to improve the community."

She gave several examples of that spirit. "When the streetcar line was extended from 39th and Bell to 45th and State Line, the men in the Annex purchased lumber and built a sidewalk up to State Line to 45th, the "end of the line." Years after the streetcars were replaced by buses and service extended, 45th and State Line was still referred to as the 'end of the line' by older residents of the area.

"In 1918 some of the men of the Annex talked to J.C. Nichols and Frank Grant of the Nichols Company about procuring city water. At that time Westwood Hills, a Nichols development, had city water purchased from Kansas City. When plans were completed for the establishment of a water company, the men of the Annex dug the ditches and laid the water lines. Each family paid $50 to join in the company which was called the Westport Annex Water Co., and still bears that name. The company is now incorporated. Our water rates started at 75 cents a month, and even with several raises, it still supplies us with water at a much lower rate than most other companies."

Both Mrs. Reynolds' husband John and her brother-in-law, William Laird, served the early government of the area. Laird was a township trustee for 18 years, before the county commissioners became the governing body of Johnson County. Reynolds was twice elected as local justice of the peace.

"In 1938 the people of Westport Annex decided they wanted sewers to take the place of existing septic tanks. A meeting was called of all the people in the school district at the school house to discuss the steps necessary to securing the sewers.

"At the meeting some of the people west of Rainbow expressed an opinion that the Annex only wanted them to come in on the plan to help pay for the sewers. John E. Reynolds (Mrs. Reynolds' husband) then made a motion to close the project to just the Annex and the motion carried. The Annex people got their sewers in at a cost of $90 a lot."

Mrs. Reynolds noted that sewer systems installed much later in other parts of the city were much more expensive. But, she added, the incident did not build any lasting ill feeling between resident groups on each side of Rainbow.

"On May 20, 1960, the Westport Annex was 'annexed' and became part of the city of Westwood. Most of the families of the former Annex are still progressive-minded, participate in community affairs, and keep their homes well-cared-for."

Ada Ketrow became Ada Reynolds in 1916 when she married John. She was then 24.

"I had gone to Kansas State Manual Training School in Pittsburg. In those days teachers didn't have to have a college degree, so I just went one term. I took the teacher's examinations and passed and then taught at Stanley. I earned $40 a month and paid $13 for room and board."

When she married, she had to quit teaching because "At that time married women were not allowed to teach." But later she taught at Hudson School in Westwood despite being married and the mother of two small children.

"They needed a teacher and my mother cared for the children during the day. By then I earned $115 a month for teaching 3rd and 4th grade. They offered me the principalship, but I felt I knew these neighborhood children too well."

"I was a teacher for four school terms at Hudson School and also the second president for the Parent Teachers' Association."

Today Mrs. Reynolds remains an active citizen and enthusiastic supporter of Westwood, very interested in its plans for the future. Her neatly kept home is decorated with the products of the twice-a-month ceramics course she attends.

She and her husband enjoyed traveling together all across the U.S. But she has never wished to live anywhere else.

"I would rather have this home here to return to than a great big beautiful home some place else."

SCHOOL LONG A CENTER

Mrs. Ada Reynolds

The school has long been a center of community activity and interests for Westwood people and its history tells much of the history of the area. Ada Ketrow Reynolds, a resident of the Westwood area since 1903, taught in the system many years ago. From her research and recollections, the following information has been compiled:

The earliest residents of Westwood and the surrounding area attended school on a now-famous historic site, the Shawnee Indian Mission grounds. Originally part of an Indian grant, these lands eventually reverted back to the government when the Indians were sent west. The Methodist mission and school begun by the Reverend Thomas Johnson stood vacant for several years.

For his work with the Indians, Thomas Johnson was given several thousand acres of land which fell to his heirs upon his death during the Civil War.

The acre on which the first school for area children was built was given for that purpose by Alexander Johnson, one of the Missionary's heirs.

Later, after redistricting, that acre was bought by a Mrs. Barbara Bescher for $300. She built the little stone bungalow later owned by Miss K.C. Roe. That attractive home still stands just east of the museum buildings on Mission Road.

On that site in 1872 a local resident named Miles Standish built the first school house to serve Shawnee Mission District No. 92. The district encompassed the area from the Johnson-Wyandotte County Line south to about 58th street, and from State Line west to about Nall Avenue.

The first school district meeting was held in the Old Mission chapel room August 22, 1873. These officers were elected: A.M. Johnson, Clerk; J.E. Bernard, Treasurer; M. Greeno, Director. Other early school board members were Miles Standish, J.G. Martin, John Swatzell Sr., Phillip Reinhardt Sr., and John Roe.

In her own words, Mrs. Reynolds describes that early school house: "The school house was a one room building with a raised platform at the front of the room where the teacher's desk stood. The room was heated by a stove in the center

Mrs. Ada Reynolds

of the room. In the small belfry above hung the bell which called the children to classes. This was the same bell used in the Indian school at the Shawnee Mission, and it now hangs among the relics in the museum there.

"The fence in front of the school was made of long iron rods between posts and the pupils entered the school yard over a stile. The drinking water was carried from the spring at the Mission.

"Miss Mitchell was probably the first teacher. The teacher's salary in those years was about $30 or $35 a month and they could procure board and lodging, including laundry, for $2 to $3 a week. In 1875 the enrollment was 51 pupils. For a good many years things went along very quietly without much change. I think for a while the attendance decreased rather than increased.

"It was about this time that the school was the social center of the neighborhood and spelling matches were in vogue. Not only the older pupils, but all the young people of the community took part in the spelling 'bees.' One year the teacher's name was Mr. Montgomery. One evening Mr. Montgomery took the Shawnee Mission spellers to Westport, Missouri, to spell against a school there. The Westport teacher's name was Mr. Lemon. The Shawnee Mission people won the spelling match, and the visitors went home shouting 'Montgomery squeezed the Lemon.'

"In about 1900 Miss Olive Crane came to District No. 92 to teach. After her death her sister Miss Mary Crane took her place and their teaching covered a span of 10 to 12 years. The Crane sisters were veteran teachers in Johnson County and considered among the best at that time. Their salaries were about $60 a month. Miss Olive once said that she began teaching school when she was young girl of 15 with her hair in a long braid down her back and some of her pupils were several years older than herself.

"When the subdivisions of Shawnee Place, Westport Annex, and Southridge began to grow, the school room became inadequate for the number of pupils. The old brick building at the Shawnee Mission, which was a blacksmith shop in the time of the Indians, still stood. After the Indians were gone and before the days of the rural mail route, this building was rented from the owner, Mr. Schleicher, and put into condition for a school room and the younger children went there for a year or two. After that the United Brethren Church building on Quapaw Street in Shawnee Place was used."

Mrs. Reynolds and her sister Anna (now Mrs. Williams Laird of Westwood) graduated from the school on the Mission grounds. Their home was just east of what is now Rainbow and it had been a long walk to school.

"My mother (Mrs. Richard Ketrow) felt that the distance to the Shawnee Mission schools was too great for small children in the Annex (area just east of Rainbow), children west of Hudson Road (now Rainbow), and children on Belinder.

"At her own expense she went to Olathe on the 'Strang Line' and learned from the county Superintendent of the Schools the necessary steps to be taken to divide the district. With the help of Mrs. Willis D. Reynolds, she circulated the necessary petition, and on August 5, 1912, the division was made and all territory east of a line halfway between Mission Road and Belinder Road was formed into School District Number 93 and called Hudson School.

"My mother was always very interested in the school and the community even though we girls were grown. I remember her saying, 'We ought to have a school of our own,' and then going out to get it. It was a lot of hard work - all those petitions, all those signatures. When they did give us our school, there was no building. But a house was being built on Hamilton (now 48th Street) and they used that 'til a building could be constructed.

"A two room brick school house was built on 48th street just west of Hudson Road. Later a room was built in the basement for the primary pupils and the intermediate and upper grades used the original rooms. Still later a two room frame building was built east of the brick building to take care of the increasing number of school children.

"After we got this school, things really started to happen here. The school was the community meeting place and many interesting programs were held there. Talented people of the district and their friends performed free of charge, and sometimes when something was needed for the school, the adults were charged ten cents, but there was never a charge for children. Teachers from Kansas University came and gave extension classes in painting, interior decorating, and sewing. Well-known book reviewers from Kansas City came to give reviews. A ten-cent charge was made for each book review given.

"In January of 1928 the school site was changed to 50th street west of Rainbow and renamed Westwood View School Number 93, and a new building built.

"In 1969 this building was torn down and a very modern, functional building was built on the same site. This new building was dedicated May 4, 1969."

The stone "W.V." from the front of the original Westwood View school building was preserved when the building was torn down. Those letters are now embedded in the north wall of the tennis court in the new mini-park at 50th and Rainbow.

Westwood's Public Servants

BEGINNING OF PUBLIC WORKS

Alley & Belinder, Summer "89

City maintenance was done by contract through private contractors for the streets, roads, sidewalks and easements. At times is was done by persons wanting to pay their court fines for a violation.

By 1989, Westwood had the most modern street cleaning and public works equipment available

The Governing Body finally made the decision to hire a man by the name of Don Graves in 1968 to perform this work with additional help as needed. Don worked for the city until April 1971 when he resigned.

During this time we had no place to store our equipment when not in use. An agreement was made with the Mobile Service Station located at Rainbow and Johnson Drive to park a dump truck and a leaf vacuum trailer there.

The City Hall had been located at the small office building on 47th Street and had moved to the Hudson Oil

Building, where the north half of their basement was to be leased as space for the city hall and police department. Also a small building was moved just back of Hudson Oil for a storage shed for small equipment the city now owned. This became the first location for the Public Works Department.

In 1971 George Brown was hired. George was a man of many talents. Not only did he supervise all the street

Public works superintendent leaves Westwood in good shape after 20 years on the job

By Jacqueline Lehatto
Sun Correspondent

When George Brown was first hired as the superintendent of the Westwood Department of Public Works he had no trouble with his staff. Of course at the time, Brown was the only employee of the Westwood Public Works Department.

Most of the work was still done by private contractors when Brown became the first DPW superintendent — and first full-time worker — 20 years ago. Last month Brown, 64, became the first superintendent to retire.

Westwood's population, 1,772 residents according to the 1990 United States census, stayed about the same while Brown ran the department. But his staff and equipment inventory grew as more municipal chores were taken over instead of contracted out.

"I've seen the time when the mayor and council would help with the leaf pickup," Brown said. "They had to, because I was by myself."

The mayor and the council limit their chores to City Hall administration now, Brown said. The department has grown to two full-time workers with part-time help in the summer.

Brown supervised street projects, drove

Sun Photo by Richard Trobaugh

RETIRING — George Brown recently retired as superintendent of Westwood's Department of Public Works.

the leaf pickup, mowed, planted, budgeted, plowed snow from streets of Westwood, Westwood Hills and Mission Woods, trimm-

ed trees, cleared streets of storm debris and fixed equipment for 20 years.

Because of the increased work load, in-

cluding the new City Hall grounds, he had to give up one of his favorite duties, doing the maintenance work on the Westwood Police Department cars.

For the last 20 years Brown has been on 24-hour emergency call, also. He lives in Kansas City, Kan., a couple of blocks from the Westwood City Hall. Many times, he said, he would report to work in the middle of the night, brought out of bed by downed trees or ice storms.

But it was being busy that Brown liked most about the job. That, and the cooperation he received from the City Council and residents.

"All the way down the line, right from the start, the council members would work with me, the mayor would work with me," Brown said. I don't ever remember being chewed out by anyone."

John Sullivan, who started with the department as a part-time worker in 1979, has taken over Brown's job.

He said he has been working hard since Brown left, especially struggling to get the landscaping equipment ready for spring clean-up. "We miss him," Sullivan said, "And we're finding it out more every day."

George Brown was the first Superintendent of the Public Works Department. He served for 20 years before retiring in 1992.

projects, road easements, and right-of-way maintenance, but took care of all repairs of the trucks, vacuums, leaf-pick-up machine, street sweeper and the police cars and their radios, etc.

He was responsible for plowing snow from the streets in Westwood, but the city had a contract with Westwood Hills and Mission Woods to take care of their roads and streets.

As more equipment was purchased a location was needed to keep the equipment inside. The city purchased the Texaco Station at 47th Street and Mission Road.

A large building on 43rd Street in Kansas City was leased for a period of time. We also kept searching for a location, even in the caves located in the City of Roeland Park. Then a opening came up behind the Fairway Hardware and we were located there for a while. From there we moved to the property known as European Motors Garage and the Phillips 66 Station.

Because of the extra work involved the city hired John Sullivan as an Assistant. Finally an opportunity came along when the property located at 2545 W. 47th Street was for sale. This property was owned by North West Central Pipe Line. The city purchased the property for $125,000 in 1986. At last we had a permanent home for the Public Works Department. This provides a place for storage, office, up-keep of all the machinery and even a concrete pad for storage of the salt and sand.

George was a very busy person for the city for 20 years when he decided to retire due to health problems. His last day was in March, 1992.

After the retirement of George Brown, John Sullivan was appointed to take over that position.

Westwood Public Works Department on West 47th Street

At this time, John is our full time superintendent and cares for this position in a very capable way, handling many projects that we require to make a successful Public Works Department.

TREE PLANTING PROGRAM

Mrs. Nancy Jeffries, Councilwoman, sponsored the Tree Planting Program when she served on the council. The Governing Body hired Mr. Max Fiebig in January 1974 to act as the Consultant in the kinds and types of trees, shrubs, flowers to be planted in the City. They felt this beauty would add character to the neighborhood and streets lined with mature healthy trees.

This program was sponsored by the Parks and Recreation Committee. The Public Works Department, though small in personnel, has done an excellent job of managing the city's public tree resource. In recognition for excellence in community forestry, Westwood has been awarded Tree City USA status.

It was found the pin oak was the most popular trees, and with five other species, comprise 60 percent of the total street tree resource. The five are sweet gum, sugar maple, green ash, Siberian elm, and silver maple. It was considered a good idea to have a variety because of the potential for insects and disease.

Many of the trees had been planted and had grown into the utility lines. This forced the trees to be topped, which produced numerous sprouts and poorly attached limbs resulting in unhealthy, unsightly trees that required constant maintenance. It was advised that the city should work closely with KCP&L to address this problem.

A goal of planting 5 new trees per year over the next five years, or 25 new trees over the next ten years, would gradually bring the stocking rate up to an ideal number.

In January and February the Public Works Department put out notices in the city newsletter reminding citizens that it is time to think about planting new trees.

Mayor Kostar, Gene Culbertson and Janet Hosty at a park dedication March 30, 1990.

They will plant a tree in a location mutually agreed upon by the owner if the owner will pay a one time $20.00 for the planting, staking, and mulching charge and agree to water, trim and otherwise properly care for the tree thereafter. There will be a choice of tree.

CITY FORESTER IS BUSY

It takes no more than a quick trip past any city property in Westwood, the mini-park, the tree-planted easements, to realize beauty is important to this city. A tour of the city's quiet neighborhoods, past the gardens and the trees, reveals an equal concern among the individual citizens.

So it comes as no surprise to learn that effective last January the city of Westwood hired a landscape consultant to plan and supervise the care of the city-owned trees, plantings, and green spaces.

The man is Max Fiebig and his work speaks for him. As building and grounds superintendent for United Telecom, Max is the man responsible for the attractive landscaping surrounding that building at Johnson Drive and Rainbow. His special pride is the corner landscaping - terraced flower beds backed by curved stone walls.

In that area Fiebig has planted 1,600 bulbs, 280 other plants, and, this spring, 3,000 annuals and 1,000 rows of zoysia. The result, he hopes, will be "an entrance to Westwood."

Fiebig has been with United Telecom for 10 years. When the utility company decided to move to Westwood, substantial funds were allotted specifically for beautification. Fiebig explained the reasoning:

"Where we were, it was deplorable. We had the idea to make our place especially beautiful, to win friends with our new neighbors in Westwood. I think we have. It did not take long."

Fiebig plans and he labors. An architect did the basic design for the company's landscaping and stonework. Fiebig did the adapting and building.

At a recent national stockholders' meeting, Fiebig was cited by the chairman of the board for his ideas and his work in the new building's attractive grounds.

In a year Fiebig will be 65 years old and he will retire from United Telecom. Westwood hired him now on a part-time consulting basis; "Then, when I retire, they say it will be up to me."

His job with the city, he explained, involves selecting trees that will be appropriate, overseeing the maintenance of city trees and plantings, and advising on future beautification plans.

So far he has been busy. In the last two years Westwood has initiated an extensive tree planting program to replace diseased trees, More than 200 trees have been planted and those young trees need care.

"They have given me the authority to select and determine how money will be spent."

On the drawing board for future landscaping plans, Fiebig said, are such projects as the extension of Belinder, hanging flower baskets along the streets, and improved alleyways. "There are many exciting plans . . . I look forward to a good association with the city in this job."

He has been involved in beautifying Westwood before, several years ago when he formed a Garden Club in the city.

Westwood's Police Department & City Officials

POLICE

On October 6, 1949, Joe Fromholz was appointed City Marshal.

He was authorized to purchase a spot light, siren, red light and an identifying sign for his car, as well as a sign to read "Police Department, City of Westwood, Kansas," and a badge for himself. Later John Grow was appointed City Marshal.

The following individuals held appointment as Police Officers:

1955
Harley Birdsong, Chief
Chesley Jones, James McCoy, Kenneth Bridgman, George Bresina, J.R. Sayre

1956 and 1957
Chesley Jones, Chief
James McCoy, Keith McVey, Vernon D. Mooney, Eldred A. Wilson, Ronnie L. Lafever, Paul E. Gant

1958 and 1959
Allen A. Wrinkle, Chief
Keith McVey, Vernon D. Mooney, Eldred A. Wilson, Robert M. Brady, M.L. Moles, Dean E. Kraisinger (reserve)

Westwood's first police car, a 1956 Ford

Police of Westwood, 1955, 1956 & 1957

1960
Allen A. Wrinkle, Chief
M.L. Moles, E.A. Wilson, Richard Tipton, M.D. Mooney

1961
A.A. Wrinkle, Chief
E.A. Wilson, M.D. Mooney, Roy F. Tipton, Jack Kirkham, Robert J. Boyce, Jens R. Lorenzen

1962
A.A. Wrinkle, Chief
E. A. Wilson, Jack Kirkham, Foy F. Stirton, Harold Hoeflicker (Reserve), James W. Melton

1963
A.A. Wrinkle, Chief
E.A. Wilson, Jack Kirkham, Roy F. Stirton, James W. Melton, Harold Hoeflicker (reserve)

1964
A.A. Wrinkle, Chief
Jack Kirkham, James Melton, Roy F. Stirton, Harold Hoeflicker, Kenneth E. Nichols (reserve)

1965
A.A. Wrinkle, Chief
Jack Kirkham, Roy F. Stirton, James Melton, Harold Hoeflicker, Kenneth E. Nichols (reserve), John W. Grist Jr. (reserve)

1966

A.A. Wrinkle, Chief

Jack Kirkham, James Melton, Fred R. Webber (reserve), Robert L. Wilson (reserve), Harold L. Hoeflicker (reserve), Roy F. Stirton (reserve)

1967

A.A. Wrinkle, Chief

Jack E. Kirkham, James Melton, Dale R. Ogran, (reserve) Fred R. Webber, Robert L. Wilson, (reserve) Jack Wise, L.E. Maloney, G.L. Neely, Chas. Rentfro

1969

A.A. Wrinkle, Chief

James Melton, Chas. Rentfro, Chas. Berry, Ronald R. Peterson (reserve), Ronald Birdsong (reserve) Dale Ogran, Thomas Seavey

1970

A.A. Wrinkle, Chief

Jim Melton, Chas. Berry, Dale Ogran, Daryl Gardner, Ron Peterson

Members of the Police Department, circa 1967

1968

A.A. Wrinkle, Chief

Jack Kirkham, James Melton, Chas. Rentfro, Fred Webber (reserve), Harold Hoeflicker (Reserve) Thomas Seavey (reserve), Charles Berry

1971

A.A. Wrinkle, Chief

James Melton, Chas. Berry, Dale Ogran, Daryl Gardner, Ron Peterson, Robert Eiden, Thomas Seavey (reserve), Richard Pressler (reserve)

1972

A.A. Wrinkle, Chief
James Melton, Dale Ogran, Daryl Gardner, Robert Eiden, Thomas Seavey (reserve), Carl Chance (reserve), Stephen Foster (reserve), Harley Sparks (Drug Abuse)

1975

A.A. Wrinkle, Chief
Robert Eiden, Dale Ogran, Carl Chance, John Cameron, Richard Allen (reserve), John Cameron, Anthony DiPlacito, Harold Hoeflicker (reserve), Ed Milan, Mike Frankovich (Drug Program County)

1973

A.A. Wrinkle, Chief
Bob Eiden, Daryl Gardner (reserve), Harley Sparks, Carl Chance, Stephen Foster (reserve), Thomas Seavey (reserve), John Cameron

1974

A.A. Wrinkle, Chief
Robert Eiden, Chas. Berry, Dale Ogran, Carl Chance, John Cameron, Harley Sparks, Anthony DiPlacito, Richard Allen

1976

Robert Eiden, Chief
Dale Ogran, Dennis Burns, John Cameron, Carlos Wells, Anthony DiPlacito, Lewis Self, Ed Milan, Mike Frankovich (Drug Squad), Harold Hoeflicker (reserve), Rick Paddock

1977

Robert Eiden, Chief
Anthony DiPlacito, Ed Milan, Dennis Burns, Lewis Self (left), Carlos Wells, Mike Frankovich (Drug Squad), Kenny Carpenter, Rick Padock, Tony Higgins

1978

Anthony DiPlacito, Chief

Kenny Carpenter, Ed. Milan (left), Dennis Burns, Carlos Wells, Tony Higgins, Don Brooks, Mike Frankovich (left), Darrell Gardner (reserve), David Letts

1979

Anthony DiPlacito, Chief

Kenny Carpenter (left), Dennis Burns (left), Carlos Wells, Don Brooks, Darrell Gardner, Tony Higgins (left), Larry Green (reserve), Greg Milan (reserve), Craig Avdeychik, Gregory Jackson

1980

Anthony DiPlacito, Chief

Carlos Wells, Craig Avdeychik, Gregory Jackson, Steve Apostle, Darrell Gardner, Greg Milan (reserve) (left), Jim Schroer (reserve), Dave Letts (reserve), Robin Shumate (reserve), Don Brooks (left)

1981

Anthony DiPlacito, Chief

Carlos Wells, Darrell Gardner, Steve Apostle (left), Jeff Roland, Jim Schroer (reserve), Robin Shumate (reserve), Leon Whitington (reserve), Dave Letts (reserve)

1982

Anthony DiPlacito, Chief

Carlos Wells, Darrell Gardner, Craig Avdeychik, Gregory Jackson, Jeff Roland, Jim Schorer (reserve), Dave Letts (reserve), Leon Whitington (reserve)

1983

Anthony DiPlacito, Chief

Carlos Wells, Craig Avdeychik, Gregory Jackson, Jeff Roland, Darrell Gardner, Dave Letts (reserve), Jim Schorer (reserve), Leon Whitington (reserve).

1984

Anthony DiPlacito, Chief

Carlos Wells, Craig Avdeychik, Gregory Jackson, Jeff Roland, Darrell Gardner, Dan Brewster, Dave Letts (left), Jim Schorer (reserve), Leon Whitington (reserve).

1985

Anthony DiPlacito, Chief (left Aug '85)

Carlos Wells, Craig Avdeychik, Gregory Jackson, Jeff Roland, Darrell Gardner, Dan Brewster, Jim Schorer (reserve), Leon Whitington (reserve)

1986

Carlos Wells, Chief

Craig Avdeychik, Gregory Jackson, Jeff Roland, Dan Brewster, Darrell Gardner, Barbara Graham, Jim Schorer (reserve), Leon Whitington (reserve)

1987

Carlos Wells, Chief

Craig Avdeychik, Gregory Jackson, Jeff Roland, Dan Brewster, Barbara Graham, Darrell Gardner, Robert Burgess, Jim Schorer (reserve), Leon Whitington (reserve)

1988

Carlos Wells, Chief

Craig Avdeychik, Gregory Jackson, Jeff Roland, Darrell Gardner, Dan Brewster, Barbara Graham, Robert Burgess, Jim Schorer (reserve), Leon Whitington (reserve)

1989

Carlos Wells, Chief

Craig Avdeychik, Gregory Jackson, Jeff Roland, Dan Brewster, Barbara Roland, Robert Burgess, Jim Schorer (reserve), Leon Whitington (reserve)

1990

Carlos Wells, Chief

Craig Avdeychik, Gregory Jackson, Jeff Roland, Dan Brewster, Barbara Roland, Robert Burgess, Phil Cross, (reserve), Jim Schorer (reserve), Leon Whitington (reserve)

1991

Carlos Wells, Chief

Craig Avdeychik, Gregory Jackson, Jeff Roland, Dan Brewster, Barbara Roland, Robert Burgess, Phil Cross (reserve), Jim Schorer (reserve), Leon Whitington (reserve)

1992

Carlos Wells, Chief

Craig Avdeychik, Gregory Jackson, Jeff Roland, Dan Brewster, Barbara Roland, Robert Burgess, Phil Cross (reserve), Jim Schorer (reserve), Leon Whitington (reserve)

1993

Carlos Wells, Chief

Craig Avdeychik, Gregory Jackson, Jeff Roland, Dan Brewster, Barbara Roland, Robert Burgess, Phil Cross (reserve) (left), Tyrone Davis (reserve), Shawn Dunn (reserve)

1994

Carlos Wells, Chief

Craig Avdeychik, Gregory Jackson, Jeff Roland, Dan Brewster, Barbara Roland, Robert Burgess, Tyrone Davis (reserve), Shawn Dunn (reserve)

1995

Carlos Wells, Chief

Craig Avdeychik, Gregory Jackson, Jeff Roland, Dan Brewster, Barbara Roland, Robert Burgess, Davis and Dunn (left)

1996

Carlos Wells, Chief

Craig Avdeychik, Gregory Jackson, Jeff Roland, Dan Brewster, Barbara Roland, Robert Burgess, Jimmy McBee (reserve), Sean McBee (reserve)

1997

Carlos Wells, Chief

Craig Avdeychik, Gregory Jackson, Jeff Roland, Dan Brewster, Barbara Roland, Robert Burgess, Jimmy McBee (reserve), Darryl Hayes (reserve), Troy Martin (reserve)

1998

Carlos Wells, Chief,

Craig Avdeychik, (retired) , Gregory Jackson, Dan Brewster, Barbara Roland, Robert Burgess, Darryl Hayes, Troy Martin, Jimmy McBee (reserve), Jeff Roland (reserve)

1999

Carlos Wells, Chief

Gregory Jackson, Dan Brewster, Barbara Roland, Robert Burgess, Darryl Hayes, Troy Martin, Don Brooks (reserve), Eric Thompson (reserve), Sean Murphy (reserve), Jeff Roland (reserve), Jimmy McBee (reserve)

Metro Squad assembled in front of Kansas City, Mo., Police Academy during training school.

The first Metro Squad, 1965. Can you find Westwood Patrollman Roy Stirton?
—Courtesy of the Kansas City, Missouri Police Department Archives

CHANGE:

Changes made at the City of Westwood following the resignation of Chief Anthony DiPlacito .

The decision was made by the Council to hire a City Administrator, Harry Malnicof was hired October 1985, a former finance director for Johnson County. He held a degree in Business administration from the National college of Business in Cedar Rapids, Iowa, primarily through extension courses.

He will take over administration functions that previously were left to the city council and Mayor.

An Ordinance was adopted outlining the duties and the authority of the new city administrator. He will also take over the duties of the police department.

According to the ordinance Mr. Malnicof will recommend appointments for removal of department heads, coordinate the work of all other departments, carry out action as directed by the council and supervise preparation of all bidding for service needed.

It turns out that the City of Westwood, with a population of 1688 according to the 1985 county census, is the smallest city in Johnson County to have a full time administrator.

Mr. Malnicof resigned in 1987.

Police Clerks
Gene Culbertson
Carol North
Diane Dory
Betty Ziegler
Jackie Blackwell
Sylvia Lopez
Lynne Pateres
Mo Hanek

Police Judges
B.N. McDonald
Norman Gaar
Joe D. Dennis
N. Jack Brown
John C. Eisele
Timothy J. Turner

City Attorneys
John R. Keach
Kenith Howard
Robert Woody
Jerry Hess
James R. Orr

City Clerks
J. E. Wilcox
Gene Culbertson
Norma Brooks
Lisa Lene
Diane Stecklin
Pam Jackson

Assistant Clerks
Gene Culbertson
Marsha Mead
Cathy Patterson
Dana Worley
Kerri Johnson
Lynn Pateres
Kathleen Patterson
Mo Hanek
Romona Clynn
Kathleen McMahon

City Treasurers
Murry Martin
Richard Tipton
Glenn Myers
Bruce Bryant
Bob Hale
Charles L. Mills

Public Works
Don Graves
George Brown
John Sullivan
Charles Stein
David Langley
Mike Ludwig

Building Inspectors
Jim Hayner
Jim Gilpin

WESTWOOD ELECTED COUNCIL

1949-1953
Mayor: Murray Maxwell,
Council: John Hearst, James Sudeath, John Kesel, Jr, Arthur Shaw, George Woster

1953-1957
Mayor: Harry Boling
Council: Joe N. Hodson, Mark Sharp

1957-1959
Mayor: Robert Fitzpatrick
Council: William "Bill" Weeks, Bert Hathaway, George Keller, Henry Strick, Buford Lutz

1959-1960
Mayor: William "Bill" Weeks
Council: Bert Hathaway, Buford Lutz, Henry Strick, Nathan L. Weis, George Keller

1960- 1963
Mayor: Buford Lutz
Council: George Keller, Lloyd Svoboda, Glenn Myers, Jean Weber, Mark Sharp

1963
Mayor: Buford Lutz
Council: Glenn Myers, Lloyd Svoboda, Mark Sharp, Jean Weber, George Keller

1964
Mayor: Norman Gaar
Council: Jean Weber, George Keller, Glenn Myers, Lloyd Svoboda, Lawrence Booker

1965
Mayor: Norman Gaar
Council: Lawrence Booker, Wm. Avery, Glenn Myers, George Keller, Lloyd Svoboda

1966
Mayor: Joe D. Dennis
Council: Wm. Avery, Lawrence Booker, George Keller, Glenn Myers, Lloyd Svoboda

1967
Mayor: Joe D. Dennis
Council: Lawrence Booker, Wm. Avery, George Keller, Richard Moore, Lloyd Svoboda

1968
Mayor: Joe D. Dennis
Council: Wm. Avery, Richard Moore, Lloyd Svoboda, Ray Johnson, George Keller

1969
Mayor: Joe D. Dennis
Council: Wm. Avery, Richard Moore, Ray Johnson, George Keller, Lloyd Svoboda

1970
Mayor: Joe D. Dennis
Council: Wm. Avery, George Keller, Ray Johnson, Richard Moore, George Kiloh

1971
Mayor: Joe D. Dennis
Council: Wm. Avery, Ray Johnson, George Keller, Richard Moore, George Kiloh

1972
Mayor: Joe D. Dennis
Council: Robert Flaspohler, Nancy Jeffries, Ray Johnson, George Kiloh, Richard Moore

1973
Mayor: Joe D. Dennis
Council: Nancy Jeffries, Robert Flaspohler, George Kiloh, Ray Johnson, Richard Moore

1974
Mayor: Joe D. Dennis
Council: Nancy Jeffries, Ray Johnson, Robert Flaspohler, Willard Oldberg, George Kiloh

1975
Mayor: Joe D. Dennis
Council: Nancy Jeffries, George Kiloh, Robert Flaspohler, Willard Oldberg, Ray Johnson

1976
Mayor: Joe D. Dennis
Council: Ray Johnson, Willard Oldberg, George Kiloh, Nancy Jeffries, Henry Strick

1977:
Mayor: Joe D. Dennis
Council: Ray Johnson, Nancy Jeffries, Henry Strick, Willard Oldberg, George Kiloh

1978
Mayor: Joe D. Dennis
Council: Ray Johnson, George Kiloh, Henry Strick, Nancy Jeffries, Willard Oldberg

1979
Mayor: Joe D. Dennis
Council: Ray Johnson, George Kiloh, Henry Strick, Willard Oldberg, Nancy Jeffries

1980
Mayor: Joe D. Dennis
Council: Nancy Jeffries, Willard Oldberg, George Kiloh, Ray Johnson, Henry Strick

1981
Mayor: Joe D. Dennis
Council: Willard Oldberg, James Foster, Henry Strick, Ray Johnson, George Kiloh

1982

Mayor: Joe D. Dennis
Council: Henry Strick, Janet Hosty, Billy Plant, Nancy Jeffries, James Foster

1983

Mayor: Joe D. Dennis
Council: Nancy Jeffries, James Foster, Janet Hosty, Billy Plant, Bill Latz

1984

Mayor Joe D. Dennis
Council: Nancy Jeffries, James Foster, Janet Hosty, Billy Plant, Bill Latz

1985

Mayor: Joe D. Dennis
Council: James Foster, Janet Hosty, Billy Plant, Bill Latz, Nancy Jeffries

1986

Mayor: Joe D. Dennis (resigned April '86)
Council: James Foster (President of the Council, became Mayor), David Enenbach, Janet Hosty, William Kostar, Bob Lindquist, Gene Culbertson

1987

Mayor: James Foster (resigned June '86)
Council: William Kostar (President of Council, became Mayor), David Enenbach, Janet Hosty, Bob Lindquist, Leroy Dykman, Gene Culbertson

1988

Mayor: William Kostar
Council: Janet Hosty, Gene Culbertson, David Enenbach, Bob Lindquist, Leroy Dykman, Gregory (Rick) Robards, (May 12th: Billy Plant appointed to fill vacated seat of Dick Donovan)

1989

Mayor: William Kostar
Council: David Enenbach, Gregory Robards, Billy Plant, Janet Hosty, Gene Culbertson

1990

Mayor: William Kostar
Council: David Enenbach, Gregory Robards, Claude Percy, Billy Plant, Gene Culbertson

1991

Mayor: William Kostar
Council: Claude Percy, Bob Dye, Vicki Ross, Billy Plant, Gregory Robards

1992

Mayor: William Kostar
Council: Bob Dye, Billy Plant, Claude Percy, Vicki Ross, Gregory Robards

1993

Mayor: William Kostar
Council: Gregory Robards, Billy Plant, Claude Percy, Vicki Ross, Bob Dye

1994

Mayor: William Kostar
Council: Vicki Ross, George Long, Claude Percy, Bob Dye, Billy Plant

1995

Mayor: William Kostar
Council: Sid Hunt, Billy Plant, Claude Percy, George Long, Dave Buck

1996

Mayor: William Kostar
Council: Billy Plant, Claude Percy, Sid Hunt, George Long, Dave Buck

1997

Mayor: William Kostar
Council: Billy Plant, Claude Percy, Sid Hunt, George Long, Dave Buck

1998

Mayor: William Kostar
Council: Billy Plant, Claude Percy, Sid Hunt, George Long, Dave Buck

1999

Mayor: William Kostar
Council: Claude Percy, Billy Plant, Dave Buck, George Long, Jim Donovan

APPENDIX

The photographs and memorabilia compiled for this book were made available by the following people and organizations

Article:	Courtesy of:
Swatzell Photos	Swatzell Family
1962 Council	*Johnson County Herald*
Westwood View Elementary	Midge Myers Miller
1940 Aerial Photo	Johnson County Archives
Green Parrot	Kansas City Museum
Hudson Oil	*Johnson County Herald*
Entercom Broadcasting	Gene Culbertson
Terrace Garden Club	Margaret Cullivan
Westwood Women's Club (2)	Marje Fey
Westwood officials with Gov. Hayden	Sun Publications, Inc.
Woodside Racquet Club	Sullivan - Culbertson
Aerial View of Woodside	Bill Plant
1989 Foundation Scholarship	Sun Publications, Inc.
1999 Foundation Scholarship	Sun Publications, Inc.
Sunshine Day School (2)	Marian Leeper
Strang Line	Shirley Stiles
Hudson School	Johnson County Museum
Westwood View School	Johnson County Museum
Pete Fordyce	Karen Johnson
Wylie V. Harris	Karen Johnson
1947 Westwood View Class Picture	Midge Myers Miller
Westwood View Graduation Card	Karen Johnson
Westwood View Staff	*Johnson County Herald*
1930 Westwood View Class Picture	Thomas Ackerman
1969 Westwood View Dedication	Karen Johnson
April Keller	April Keller
William Weeks	William Weeks
Norman E. Gaar	Norman E. Gaar
Joe Dennis	Joe Dennis
William L. Kostar	William L. Kostar
Marcus Pasley	Marcus Pasley
Old Car	Pasley Family
Case Tractor	Pasley Family
Chief Al Wrinkle	Wrinkle Family
Ranger Membership Card	Wrinkle Family
Guaranteed Foods	*The Scout*
Mr. & Mrs. Wrinkle	Wrinkle Family
Boys Club (2)	Wrinkle Family
Mrs. Eileen Wrinkle (2)	Wrinkle Family
Ray Johnson	Election Notice
Sprint Corporate Headquarters	Sprint
4740 Rainbow (2)	Keller Family
Woodside Racquet Club	Gaar - Dennis - ? - Sullivan - Culbertson
Fairway Shopping Center	Johnson County Museum

Pebble Horn	Pebble Horn
The Myers Home	Norma Jean Taylor Donnell
"Downhome"	Thomas Ackerman
Westwood View Class	Thomas Ackerman
Marjorie Theis Jett	Thomas Ackerman
The Ackerman Cousins	Thomas Ackerman
The Cullivan Train	Cullivan Family
Hudson School	Johnson County Museum
Kansas Retail Cigarette License	Lyle Wrightsman
Bell Memorial Hospital	KU Archives
Saying Goodbye	Sun Publications, Inc.
Mr. & Mrs. Nick Fromholz	Sun Publications, Inc.
Mr. & Mrs. William Laird	Sun Publications, Inc.
Mrs. Ada Reynolds	Sun Publications, Inc.
Alley & Belinder	Sun Publications, Inc.
Street Sweeper	Sun Publications, Inc.
George Brown	Sun Publications, Inc.
Public Works Department	Sun Publications, Inc.
Park Dedication	Sun Publications, Inc.
First Police Car	Sun Publications, Inc.
Westwood Police, 1955`	Mrs. Chesley Jones
Westwood Police, 1967	Mrs. Eileen Wrinkle
Westwood Police	Mrs. Eileen Wrinkle
First Metro Squad	Kansas City Police Archives
Harry Malincof	Sun Publications, Inc.

SUN NEWSPAPERS ARTICLES

Hudson Oil Property
Westwood Neighborhood Association
Association Plays a Major Role
Foundation Promotes City
Westwood Foundation Scholarships
New Executive Director
Oldest Business Predates City
Westport Annex Water Company History
Older Residents
Former Official Sees Change
School Long A Center
Public Works Superintendent
Tree Planting Program
City Forester is Busy
Police

About the Author

Ms. Gene Culbertson moved to Kansas City, Kansas, with her husband, Otto, and daughter, Kay, in 1945. The young family lived for a short period of time near 7th and Central, but soon found themselves living in the Quindaro Homes area. Their house payment was $30 per month and included all expenses, maintenance, and yard upkeep.

During the next eight years the family grew to include a second daughter, Linda, and a son, Gary. This caused the family to look for a larger house. Otto found one he liked and put a $5.00 deposit down and promised to return the next day to have Gene look and approve. That night, however, his boss called and offered to sell him a vacant lot next to the house he was to show Gene the next day. The Culbertson family lost their deposit and purchased the lot for $1,200.

Within months the house was built and the family occupied it in the spring of 1953. Gene grew to love the house, its location, and the interesting events that soon occurred. The most memorable one happened soon after they moved into the house. It was nearing supper time and Gene could not find the kids. She walked up the street to Belinder and rounded the corner. She soon found the kids on the farm located at present day 50th Terrace and Belinder. The kids thought that they had moved to heaven.

Gene Culbertson

The kids grew and attended Westwood View Grade School, located right next door. Even today, Gene thinks that the best asset to the neighborhood is the school located next door.

Like the Culbertson's, Westwood was growing up too. Gene answered a phone call one day and was ultimately asked to temporarily assist City Clerk Wilcox - to help him get caught up in the paperwork. This temporary job led to Gene being appointed City Clerk in 1968. She held that position until her retirement in the fall of 1983. In that time span, Gene proved herself a force to be reckoned with, an asset to the community, a friend, an ally, and perhaps the single most important force that helped Westwood become the community it is today.

Gene's retirement did not last long. In August of 1985 she was asked to fill a vacated seat on the city council. Gene was elected to the same seat in 1986. She retired, again, in 1990. Since that time she has been active with the Westwood Foundation, the Garden Club, the Women's Club, Westwood Christian Church, and many other civic organizations.

In the fall of 1998 she was asked to help coordinate a book commemorating Westwood's History. She initially hesitated, but agreed to do so. Who better to coordinate the book than the person that has been a vital asset to her community for over five decades.

4704 Adams

The home of Charles and Ida Belle (James) Ackerman, 4704 Adams, Westwood, Kansas, circa 1915.

Another view in front of 4704 Adams. The house across the street belonged to the Metcalfs. The Westwood City Hall now stands on this property. Maribelle McCelland Waid stands on the running board beside her dad, Uncle Martin.

Annual, traditional 4th of July picnic in the back yard downhome at Grammies. We had an old wooden table we got out of the garage for the occasion.. Seated left to right: Tommie Stratton, friend; Aunt Ruth McCelland; Grammie (Ida Belle Ackerman); Mary Thies Jewell; Marjorie Thies Jett; Barbara Ackerman Fadler; Mary Ellen Park, friend.

Standing left to right: Alice Ackerman Stedman; a friend; Alfred Thies (my dad); Faye Thies (my mom); Tom Stratton, friend; J. B. Waid; Maribelle McCelland Waid; Tom Ackerman; Ken Scherrer; Virginia Thies Scherrer; Gertrude Park, friend. This was probably on July 4, 1939. (Aunt Marianna Ackerman no doubt was taking the picture.)

Wild Rose Farm near present day 50th Terrace and Belinder, Westwood

2903 W. 51st Terrace

The Beilharz home was
built in 1935.
It was the second house
on the street.

Gollob Beilharz moved into the
home with his bride, Sarah, after
their honemoon.

Gollob Beilharz was a cabinet
maker. Sarah taught & cooked
at a school.

112

Aerial view. Mission Road on the left, 51st Street Terrace on the bottom, 51 Street Middle, 50th Terrace as a dead end. Wild Rose Farm would be to the right (East) of the cul-de-sac.. Photo taken after

113

Allen's Drive-in circa 1950

Allen's Drive-in circa 1957

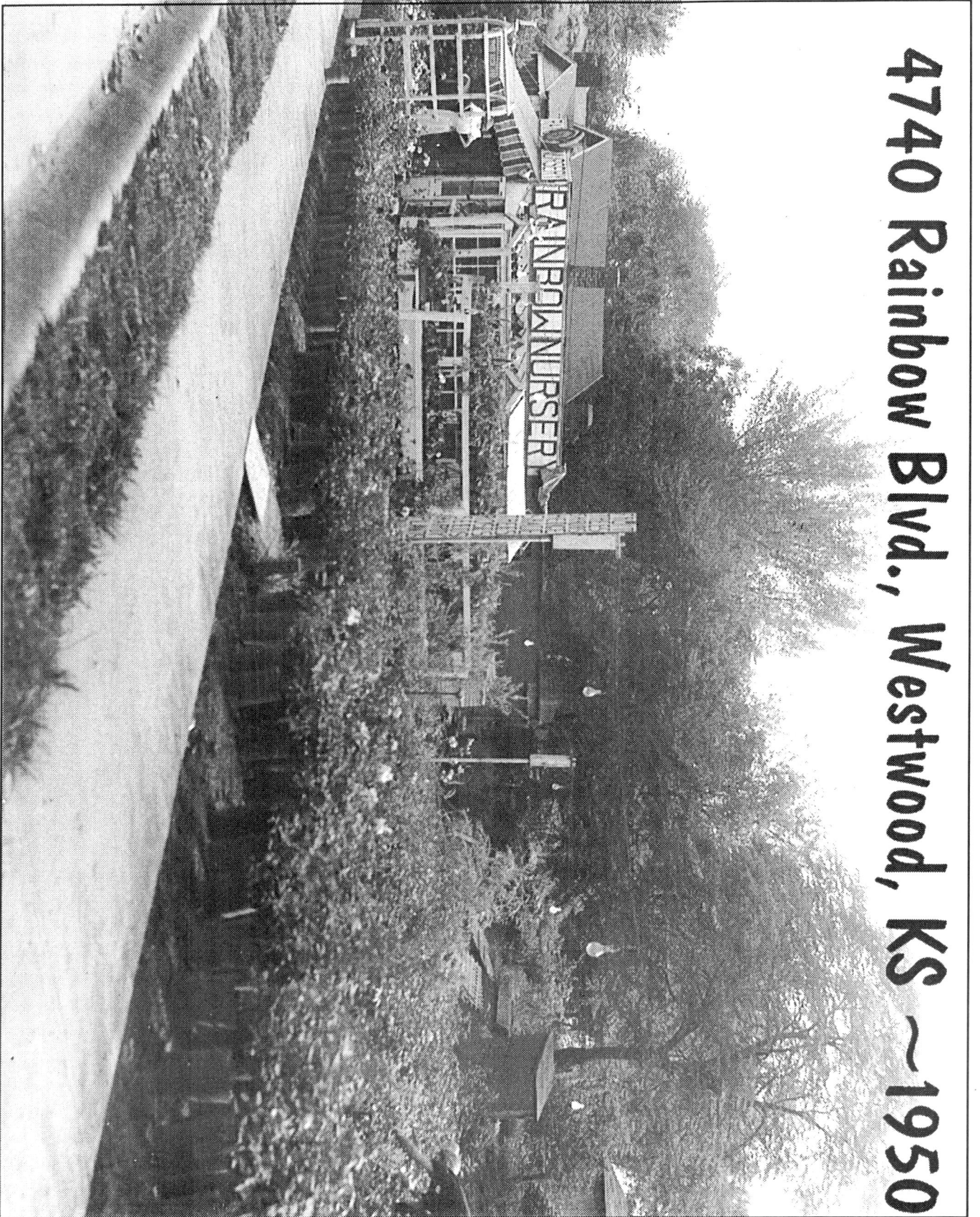

4740 Rainbow Blvd., Westwood, KS ~1950

Westwood's 25th Anniversary Parade, 1974

Driving:
Ray Johnson
Left to right:
Robert Flashpohler,
Willard Oldberg,
Nancy Jefferies.

Unknown Marching Band

1981 Elected Council

Left to right: Henry Strick, Willard Olberg, Joe Dennis (Mayor), Bob Hale (City Treasurer), James Foster, Ray Johnson, Gene Culbertson (City Clerk).

GRAND OPENING — On hand for the ribbon cutting of the United Supers grocery store which opened in place of the Westwood A&P on 47th Street Thursday were (left to right front row): Lynn Wiggins (co-owner of United Super), Joe Dennis (mayor of Westwood), Alan Wiest (co-owner of United Super), Debbie Wiest, Jean Culbertson (city treasurer of Westwood), Elinor Couch; (back row), James Foster (Westwood City Council), Willard Oldberg (Westwood City Council), Jim Yates (Retail Grocers Association), Henry Strick (Westwood City Council), Jim Sheehan (Retail Grocers Association), George Kiloh (Westwood City Council), and Byron Duffield (president of Fleming Foods Co. Kansas City Division).

April, 1982

CHRISTMAS IN WESTWOOD — George Brown and John Sullivan cut supports for a city Christmas tree they're setting up in Westwood City Park, 50th Street and Rainbow Boulevard. The city hopes to start an annual tradition with its first tree this year. The Bill Taylor household, 2623 W. 47th Terrace, donated the tree after deciding to relandscape the yard, and A.L. Muehlberger Concrete Construction provided transportation. No ceremony is planned, but about 300 lights on the tree are to be turned on today.

1990 Park Dedication, 47th Terrace

Left to right: Claud Percy, John Sullivan, Janet Hosty, Gene Culbertson, Bill Koster, George Brown

The Sun Newspapers April 29, 1992

WESTWOOD OFFICIAL HONORED — John Sullivan, Westwood's public works director, is the 1992 recipient of the Kansas State Forester's Award.

120

Photo by Hattie Akers-Barham

DIGGING OUT — Westwood city workers Michael Ludwig and Josh Thompson try to keep up with Mother Nature by cleaning the snow off the steps at the Westwood City Hall during the snowstorm early Wednesday.

Charlotte Moidl's Easter egg tree.

Star Magazine, March 25, 1990

Charlotte Moidl poses with some of the rabbit in her collection that draws hundreds of visitors to her home in Westwood each spring and has earned her the title of the Easter Lady.

121

Preparations for the foundation of Westwood City Hall

Completed City Hall